A Right to Housing?

A Right to Housing?

Samuel Stein

VERSO
London • New York

First published by Verso 2026

The manufacturer's authorized representative in
the EU for product safety (GPSR)
is LOGOS EUROPE, 9 rue Nicolas Poussin, 17000, La Rochelle, France
Contact@logoseurope.eu

1 3 5 7 9 10 8 6 4 2

Verso
UK: 6 Meard Street, London W1F 0EG
US: 207 East 32nd Street, New York, NY 10016
versobooks.com

Verso is the imprint of New Left Books

ISBN-13: 978-1-8367-4326-2
ISBN-13: 978-1-8367-4328-6 (US EBK)
ISBN-13: 978-1-8367-4327-9 (UK EBK)

British Library Cataloguing in Publication Data
A catalogue record for this book is available from the British Library

Library of Congress Cataloging-in-Publication Data

Names: Stein, Samuel author
Title: A right to housing? / Samuel Stein.
Description: London; New York: Verso, 2026. | Includes bibliographical references.
Identifiers: LCCN 2026006534 (print) | LCCN 2026006535 (ebook) | ISBN 9781836743262 paperback | ISBN 9781836743286 ebook
Subjects: LCSH: Housing | Human rights
Classification: LCC HD7287 .S755 2026 (print) | LCC HD7287 (ebook) | DDC 363.5--dc23/eng/20260325
LC record available at https://lccn.loc.gov/2026006534
LC ebook record available at https://lccn.loc.gov/2026006535

Typeset in Sabon MT by Hewer Text UK Ltd, Edinburgh
Printed and bound by CPI Group (UK) Ltd, Croydon CR0 4YY

For my mother, Penney Stein,
sower of the gardener's optimism

Amazing, that something as tiny, really, as the self should contain contending subselves—and that these subselves should themselves be constructed of subselves, and on and on and on.

—Philip Roth

In my reassessments, he said, I have lost my bearings, and I will have to find new ones.

—Rachel Kushner

Contents

Preface

It's a hard time to be. Wisdom and foolishness; belief and incredulity; we have everything before us and we have nothing before us. It clearly is the worst of times, but, in some small ways, it might also be the best.

One of the many forces behind these feelings is the persistent and pervasive housing question—its price, its availability, its quality, its control. Rents are excessive, buildings are decaying, and homelessness is reaching historic heights. Everywhere we turn, housing is an urgent issue in local and national politics, in micro- and macro-economics, and in even our most personal deliberations.

Innovative and inspiring organizing is ascendant across the country and around the world, from autonomous tenant unions battling landlords at the building and neighborhood scales to local and national coalitions fighting for comprehensive political change. In my home city and state of New York, the housing movement is riding a wave of organizing and political victories, having pushed the legislature to strengthen tenants' rights several times over and fielded a winning mayoral candidate on a platform of freezing rents and building social housing. In his general election victory speech, after opening with a Eugene Debs quote, Mayor-elect Zohran Mamdani pledged, "We will hold bad landlords to account because the Donald Trumps of our city have grown far too comfortable taking advantage of their tenants."

But even as this self-activity arises, there is evermore cause for concern, based not only on the facts of the present but also on the prospects for the future. As I write these words, the president of the United States has sent troops to occupy several cities and warned of an even greater escalation to come. He called New York's next mayor "A COMMUNIST" (pejoratively), threatening to starve our city of federal funds and flood our streets with immigration police. In this world gone mad, many—myself very much included—feel wrecked and wracked by compounding crises, even as we work to repair the world.

In the midst of all this tumult, I was invited to deliver a discourse on "Architecture and the Right to Housing in New York City" to a gathering of activists, designers, and scholars. I was excited for the opportunity to think through the concept of "a human right to housing," a framework that my comrades and I often assert as a fact, even as the facts on the pavement clearly suggest otherwise. But I did not feel up to the task of delivering an energetic and inspiring speech. Too much in the world seemed too terrible to summon an unflinchingly optimistic spirit. I could not shake the urge to express something else—an impulse born not only out of the present conjuncture but from a deeper understanding of what we're up against. I was not giving up, and never would, but I could not say I possessed the elusive quality of *hope* that is so central to our political discourse. This structure of feeling was not mine alone, I sensed, but a part of something bigger.

And so, rather than sublimate the grim to the sanguine, I pledged to write both the encouraging speech I would go on to deliver as well as a more despairing version I would not, and present the two side by side as coequal truths: a genuine, heartfelt explication of the ways we could secure and deliver a universal right to housing in our cities, opposite an equally genuine and heartfelt exploration of why it is so hard to envisage such a program coming to fruition. Certain themes, phrases, figures, and ideas would echo asynchronously across these parallel addresses, revealing different meanings in their divergent contexts. At a time when many are grasping for solutions to vexing social, economic, and political problems like the perpetual housing crisis, and yet are increasingly disillusioned with governments, parties, and legacy social-movement formations, these works would honor these conflicting sentiments by formally exhibiting the Gramscian dialectic between pessimism of the intellect and optimism of the will.

They begin as one, with "A Human Right?," an introductory framing of the concept of a right to housing, its history, and its centrality as a demand in contemporary urban political movements. From there, the text splits into two parallel parts.

One part, titled "We Can," is an earnest engagement with a right to housing in New

York, and forms the core of the address I would offer at the architects' gathering. It grapples with the meaning of a right to housing and its component parts—a right to shelter, a right to a home, and a right to the city—and it dives deep into the campaigns the city's tenant and homeless movements are waging to transform this right from rhetoric to reality.

The other, titled "Can We," is an unflinching inquiry into whether our system could truly support a universal right to housing and why our institutions balk at the prospect of providing decommodified housing for all. Deeper still, this section seeks to understand the left's declining faith in radical alternatives born of struggle and victory, paired with its admirably unyielding commitment to continue fighting nonetheless—a combination of tendencies I name "nihilism of the intellect, naivety of the will."

I aimed to somehow draw those two byways together into a common conclusion, which might hold different valences in light of the contrasting versions of the lecture that precede it. The closing to the book, in both its optimistic and pessimistic sides, is titled "Doubt and Faith," and it presents words of wisdom from some of my communal leaders, who have, in recent years, encouraged an ethic of ongoing and heightened struggle despite any feelings of hopelessness or helplessness we may harbor. It might not resolve the question of housing as a human right, as that question may not be resolvable at present, but it closes on a note of resoluteness, regardless.

Inception, divergence, reunion: this unconventional narrative format might be more easily grasped through a schematic.

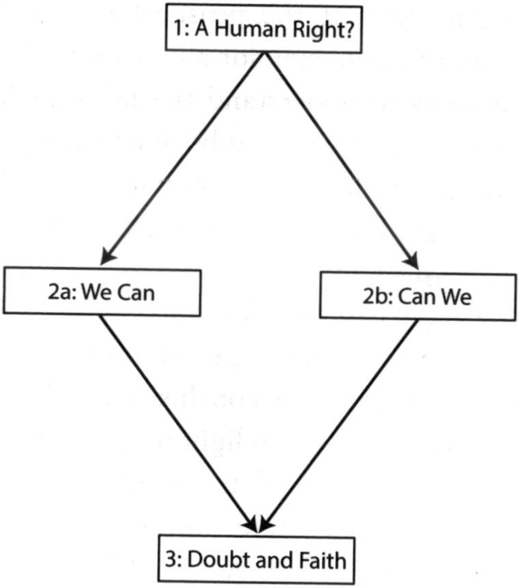

The first person I pitched this idea to was my friend Rami Younis, a Palestinian journalist who cowrote and codirected the documentary *Lyd* with my wife, Sarah Ema Friedland. They call their film a "speculative documentary" because it both depicts the city of Lyd as it exists today and also uses various filmic techniques to show the same place as it might have been had history gone differently. When I described to Rami the split structure I aimed to devise, he exclaimed, "It's a speculative speech!"

And so it is. While I have not generally gravitated toward the "speculative craze" in contemporary political storytelling, as my friend David Greenberg called it in a shared moment of exasperation, I seem to have reproduced it here. This suggests there is something in this wild world that is pulling us toward the unfamiliar. Strange as it might be, I am running with the impulse to reject the choice between agency and structure, enthusiasm and dejection, faith and doubt, the desperate existential need for a better future and the increasingly dire circumstances in which we live.

I could pathologize this impulse as a split in my personality, but I choose instead to view it as a manifestation of something more universal.

While some of us might lean more in one direction than the other, or might present one side in public and the other in private, I believe that the duality I offer in this book expresses a common condition, particularly in these perilous times.

I have never studied psychology, but a therapist once told me that the mind is more like a head of garlic than an onion: rather than peeling back the layers to expose a rich singular core, we remove the skin to find separate but connected spheres, coexisting distinctly while forming a larger whole. The part of myself that fights every day for a real right to housing and to transform society out of its capitalist rut stands beside the segment that questions whether the state and society as we know it could even deliver such a right, and whether we will be able to build a new world before the one we inhabit becomes hopelessly inhospitable.

On the Jewish holiday of Passover, we recite questions asked through the personages of four archetypal children: the wise child, the wicked child, the simple child, and the child who does not yet know how to inquire. In some traditions and prayer guides, these children are not meant to be understood as separate individuals or character types ranked by their proclivities and piousness, but rather to represent characteristics we all hold, either simultaneously or at different stages of life. We are all wise; we are all wicked; we are all simple; we are all ignorant.

Likewise, we who feel the weight of the world and are compelled to relieve it are propelled by a faith in our collective ability to build power and remake the conditions we live and labor under. At the same time, we are haunted by a fear that the chasm between the systems we can devise and the world we have inherited are too vast, and that our structural analyses of why things are the way they are may be built on firmer ground than our visionary projections of how we want them to be. We are the optimistic child and the pessimistic child; the naive child and the nihilistic child. To be an activist, an organizer, a radical, or a revolutionary is to inhabit both conditions at once, and to dwell in the discomfort of this duality. Without this orientation, neither a sober understanding of the world we inhabit nor a drive to transform it can be sustained.

I wrote the first draft of this manuscript in New York City between Juneteenth and Labor Day 2025, and the context of those ten weeks undoubtedly shaped the book's contents. The epigraphs leapt out at me from two of the novels I read as I was writing. The tone reflects some of the mostly—but not exclusively—awful events in the news: the never-ending stream of affronts emanating from the capital and the ongoing war crimes in Gaza, Sudan, Ukraine, and elsewhere; but also the surprise surge and victory of a socialist candidate in the New York City mayoral primary—and later, as I was editing, in the general election.

These events, even when not explicitly alluded to in the text, contribute to the ambient air of uncertainty over the present and the future alike. As bad as things have become, little is predictable. Will the world stand up against nationalist furor and wannabe führers, or will it fall to the forces of fascism? Will the young democratic socialist mayor of the largest US city live up to the expectations he raised and enact his ambitious agenda, or will he be thwarted by the white supremacists in the White House and the extreme centrists in the statehouse? We do not know, and we will not until today becomes tomorrow's yesterday.

I intend for this book to be both a topical intervention into the current chaos as well as a lasting contribution to the socialist struggle, particularly in the ever-pressing arena of housing. I hope that the ideas and platforms discussed in "We Can" help fuel the movement for social housing, and that the thoughts and concerns expressed in "Can We" help explain why definitive victories remain remote.

This moment calls for an escalation in dissent, even as it also provokes an escalation in despair. We wish for things to get better, and we fear that they will not. We will not get through this time by embracing one and shunning the other, but by honoring them as coequal impulses and giving each their due. Optimism versus pessimism is a far less determinative distinction than determination versus resignation.

A right to housing is possible, but—like so much else that lies at the core of a better society—it will never be achieved by ignoring the reasons why today, in New York, in the United States, and in most of the world, it eludes us. It is one thing to chant that housing is a human right; it is another thing entirely to secure and sustain it. That takes organizing, solidarity, discipline, and creativity. It takes ongoing commitment, even—indeed especially—after power is won and rights are enumerated. It demands clarity about the ways of the world, confidence in our analysis, and courage to act on our convictions. And even with all these demanding qualities in our grasp, success is never guaranteed.

Optimistically, in the future, this book will become an artifact of a worse time, when the titular question mark was still obligatory because life's necessities were treated as an array of accumulation strategies. Pessimistically, it will remain relevant as the status quo carries on, or it will be forgotten for failing to predict just how bad our collective condition could become. In the meantime, we press on, entirely uncertain of what it is ahead.

Onward.

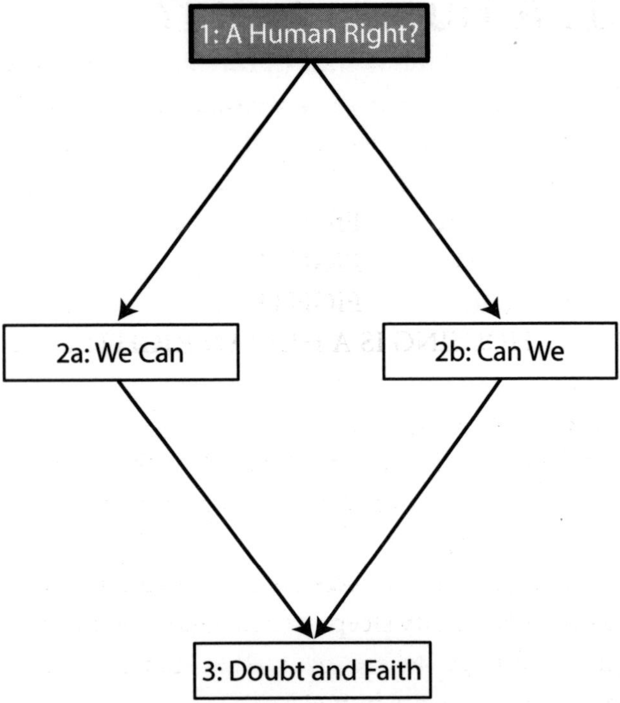
1: A Human Right?
2a: We Can
2b: Can We
3: Doubt and Faith

1. A Human Right?

FIGHT!
FIGHT!
FIGHT!
HOUSING IS A HUMAN RIGHT!

Is it?

What does it mean that we chant these words at nearly every single housing demonstration in a city where each night—as of summer 2025, when I am writing these words—over 100,000 people in New York City sleep in homeless shelters,[1] and in a country where over three-quarters of a million people are homeless?[2]

Is the human right to housing backed by local, state, national, or international law? If so, how is it being so flagrantly flouted?

If a right is something you are actionably entitled

to do or have, does the right to housing still exist absent the ability to wield it? Can rights endure without state power (or some other source of collective control) to enact and enforce them?

Is housing a natural right? Is it a right granted by the divine? If housing—like everything else we need to live in this world, including healthcare, food, water, air, and so on—is a human right, whose responsibility is it to provide and protect it, and therefore who, exactly, is letting us down?

Does couching the right to housing as a *human* right relegate it to the realm of the abstract and aspirational, rather than the real and present? Does it add validity to our claim, or does it remind us of all the other supposedly universal human rights our sovereigns regularly deny to portions of their populations?

Can we summon a right through incantation? Does repeating this mantra build meaning and strength over time, or does it devolve into a ritualized performance?

Can we conjure this right into existence through the moral force of our convictions? Does a right exist because it should?

These questions rush through my mind every time I hear those words chanted—which is to say many times a month, sometimes more than once daily, depending on the cadence of our campaigns.

Perhaps the word that challenges me the most in this chant is the simplest of them all: "is." When we shout that housing *is* a human right—not just that housing *should be* a human right, or that we're fighting to *make* housing a human right—we are saying that this right exists *NOW*, and the extreme housing inequities we face are therefore a severe violation of our human rights.

There are legal statutes of various kinds that justify this claim. Certainly under United Nations international law, housing is included in the core bundle of human rights. The Universal Declaration of Human Rights, adopted in 1948, declares in Article 12 that "no one shall be subjected to arbitrary interference with his [*sic*] privacy, family, home or correspondence" and that "everyone has the right to the protection of the law against such interference or attacks." In Article 25, the declaration establishes that "everyone has the right to a standard of living adequate for the health and well-being of himself and of his family, including food, clothing, housing and medical care." Furthermore, the 1966

International Covenant on Economic, Social and Cultural Rights establishes that signatories "recognize the right of everyone to an adequate standard of living for himself [*sic*] and his family, including adequate food, clothing and housing, and to the continuous improvement of living conditions."

This is at once an incredibly idealistic and yet deeply limited framework. Its power lies in its radical universality: These rights are assigned to *everyone*, across time and space, stretching even into the future in the 1966 covenant's commitment to "continuous improvement." It is meant to establish a baseline standard of living that all nations must strive toward, leaving no one behind.

But the Universal Declaration's approach to the right to housing is a negative right against arbitrary eviction and a positive right to a wage high enough to pay for housing; it is not a commandment to its signatories that they enact binding enforcement mechanisms, nor does it compel them to build the housing that human rights law establishes we all must be able to afford and remain within. The covenant takes a step closer to mandating state action by asserting that "States Parties will take appropriate steps to ensure the realization of this right," but this leaves a great deal to interpretation, and even to willful failure. The United States became a signatory to the covenant in 1977 (though the Senate has since refused to ratify it). Since 1980, US homelessness has grown by about 500 percent,[3] while the overall population has increased by just over 50 percent, and public housing production has cratered amid programs for demolition and privatization.[4]

The US constitutional order is largely premised on negative rights—in other words, protections from the government (often specifically private property rights), as opposed to positive rights to material goods. But while US policy has largely been hostile to housing as a human right, there have been points at which we came closer to establishing and safeguarding it. As W. E. B. DuBois chronicled in *Black Reconstruction in America,* radical reconstructionists often included land and housing redistribution as a core part of their revolutionary program. In his famous "Second Bill of Rights" address in 1944, Franklin Delano Roosevelt declared "the right of every family to a decent home" had become self-evident, regardless of "station, race, or creed."[5]

Five years later, and seven months after the Universal Declaration of Human Rights was proclaimed, the US signed into law the Housing Act of 1949. Section 2 of the law establishes a National Housing Goal:

> The Congress hereby declares that the general welfare and security of the Nation and the health and living standards of its people require housing production and related community development sufficient to remedy the serious housing shortage, the elimination of substandard and other inadequate housing through the clearance of slums and blighted areas, and the realization as soon as feasible of the goal of a decent home and a suitable living environment for every American family, thus contributing to the development and redevelopment of communities and to the advancement of the growth, wealth, and security of the Nation.

This being America, the next sentence of the statute completely undermines the first and points us in extremely limited directions guided primarily by the profit-seeking private housing industry: "The Congress further declares that such production is necessary to enable the housing industry to make its full contribution toward an economy of maximum employment, production, and purchasing power." The law then lists the policy's objectives, in an ordering that reflected and enshrined the political economy of housing in the US: "(1) private enterprise shall be encouraged to serve as large a part of the total need as it can; (2) government assistance shall be utilized where feasible to enable private enterprise to serve more of the total need." Only *after* private enterprise and government action in service of real estate do we arrive at any stipulation for local authorities to build public housing, with the aid of the national government in clearing "slums and blighted areas."[6]

This was not the only vision for housing rights in the US, though—it is just the vision that won. The 1949 Housing Act codified the result of fights over two competing versions of housing policy from the previous decade. On the left flank was the Labor Housing Conference, a group of social democratic unions and urbanists, which called on the state to support labor and other social movement organizations in building housing for the broad working class (from the destitute to the upwardly mobile) on vacant land in and around cities and towns.[7] On the right flank was the National Public Housing Conference, made up of a strange amalgam of groups like the National Association of Real Estate Brokers and nonprofit reformers, which called on the state to demolish substandard housing and replace it with public housing exclusively for the poor.[8] The Labor Housing Conference pitched their model as a threat to the reign of private developers over the housing system; the National Public Housing Conference framed their preferred policy as complementary to the private sector, which, they argued, was uninterested in or unable to build for the immiserated urban poor.[9]

While the early New Deal experimented with a program much closer to the Labor Housing Conference model, developing some of the finest public housing in the country under the auspices of the Public Works Administration, Congress ultimately adopted the National Public Housing Conference's bulldoze-first approach, setting off an era of mass urban demolition and subsidized suburban sprawl under the Federal Housing Administration, or FHA—a group whose mission the Labor Housing Conference mocked as "Fuck Housing Altogether."[10]

As a result, the country's de facto housing policy became miserly public housing and expansive private development subsidy—less a dual market than a dialectic; in Keeanga-Yamahtta Taylor's words, "a single United States housing market that was defined by its racially discriminatory, tiered access—each tier reinforcing and legitimizing the other."[11]

But this was not the end of the struggle. A right to housing was a core element of the civil rights movements, although the demands for civil and political rights are generally emphasized in the historical memory over demands for material redistribution and public sector expansion. Figures like Bayard Rustin, A. Philip Randolph, Martin Luther King, and Corretta Scott King collaborated with union leaders and progressive economists to craft the Freedom Budget for All Americans, which in 1966 called for not only full employment and the total eradication of poverty, but also a universal right to housing. Point four of its seven-point plan set out to "*wipe out slum ghettos* and provide decent homes for all Americans" (emphasis in the original).[12]

This is an interesting formulation, worth dwelling on for a moment. The Freedom Budget embraced elements of the two political poles of the 1930s public housing movement: the right-leaning National Public Housing Conference's commitment to "slum clearance" and the left-leaning Labor Housing Conference's commitment to open access. It did not romanticize "slum ghettos" but rather called for their replacement by generous social housing for all.

The document's primary author, Bayard Rustin, lived in exactly this kind of housing from 1962 to 1987, much of that time with his partner Walter Naegle.[13] Penn South, the social housing development Rustin and later Naegle called home, is cherished today as one of the outstanding achievements of the twentieth-century labor movement in New York: a campus built by the garment workers union's housing fund that spans twenty acres of central Manhattan. Its fifteen buildings average twenty-one stories and contain 2,820 apartments. Rustin was the first resident of his apartment in building 7B, and he likely considered it an inspiration for the national program he pursued.[14]

While the Freedom Budget was never adopted, the fight for a right to housing in America has continued. Recently, tenant and homeless organizations have fought for a "Homes Guarantee," a platform that includes rent controls, eviction protections, and the construction of mass social housing on a scale unseen in this country for fifty years. It found a champion in Bernie Sanders's presidential campaigns and has continued at the local level in cities and states thereafter.

Although a right to housing feels fairly distant in New York City today, it is absolutely possible to conceptualize how it could work and what it might take to enforce it. According to sociologist Mary Pattillo, eighty-four countries include some degree of housing rights in their governing constitutions, with nations like postapartheid South Africa perhaps going the furthest to enshrine—if not necessarily to deliver—a human right to housing.[15] American legal scholar Fran Quigley argues that the negative rights enshrined in the US Constitution are unachievable without positive human rights and are therefore interdependent with the right to housing.[16]

In 1989, the Institute for Policy Studies' Working Group on Housing released *The Right to Housing: A Blueprint for Housing the Nation*, which spelled out the ills of the current system and called for a mix of affordable housing preservation, rental and ownership subsidies, and affordable housing construction, which would cost roughly the equivalent of what the federal government already spent on tax breaks for rich homeowners.[17] Rachel G. Bratt, Michael E. Stone, and Chester Hartman's collection *A Right to Housing: Foundation for a New Social Agenda* updated this vision for the twenty-first century.[18]

Four years ago, my friend Rob Robinson, a formerly homeless activist for housing and human rights in New York City and around the world, coauthored an op-ed with Jessica Katz, then the executive director of the centrist New York think tank Citizens Housing and Planning Council, titled "Taking 'Housing Is a Human Right' from Slogan to Reality."[19] The two of them have shared a long "odd couple" relationship of mutual respect, despite Rob's prominence as a radical and Katz's reputation as a reformer. Written at the moment when New York City was moving homeless New Yorkers back into shelters after temporarily housing them in far safer and more dignified hotel rooms during the COVID lockdown, their joint statement called for universalizing federal rental assistance for all who qualify, exempting affordable housing production from lengthy and often contentious public review, and lessening the burden on the poor to repeatedly prove their eligibility for every assistance program.

More recently, a collective from the 2024 Big Swings fellowship sponsored by the Urban Design Forum proposed that New York enshrine housing as a human right in our state constitution. Framed as a means to universalize housing rights rather than protect them for particular and thus exposed groups—namely recently arrived immigrants—the group recommended that this new right encompass everything from eviction protections and income-based rents to habitability, accessibility, siting standards, and cultural competency. The state would be equally responsible for respecting, protecting, and fulfilling this compound and complex right. In a discussion following their presentation, the fellows clarified that while declaring a constitutional right would not necessarily make it so, such an action would give housing movements a legal lever to demand more and better from the state.

Pie in the sky? Perhaps. That phrase, though,

comes from an old Wobblies song by Joe Hill, which warns its listeners not to fall for promises of dessert in the afterlife from those who starve you in the present. In its original sense, then, the right to housing is only "pie in the sky" if it is promised as something that will be delivered to you in the distant future, premised on your good behavior in the here and now. If, however, it is presented as part of a *fight*—as the opening words of the housing movement's chant insist—then it is something else entirely: a visible political horizon for struggles in the immediate present.

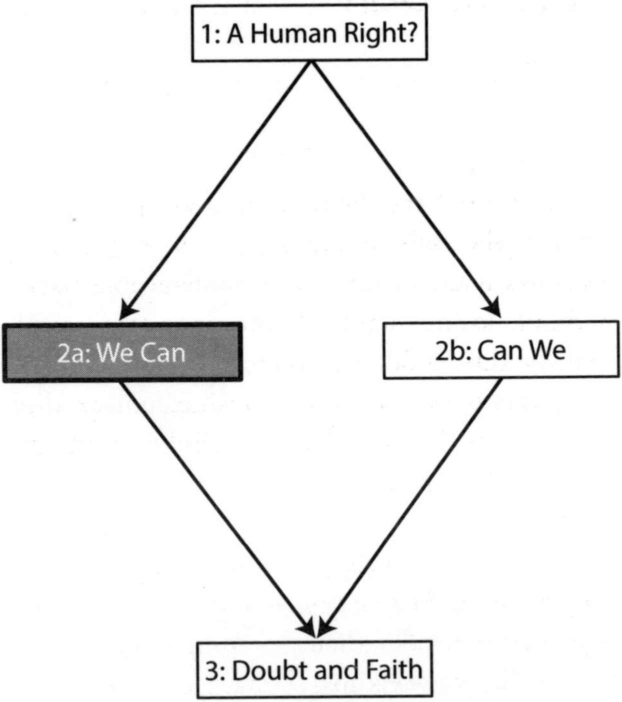
1: A Human Right?
2a: We Can
2b: Can We
3: Doubt and Faith

2a. We Can

We can move from the right to housing as a principle to the right to housing as a program by breaking it down into more manageable parts, without losing sight of the long-term goal. Usually this is done through the characteristic components of a right to housing: universality, affordability, habitability, accessibility, mobility, and so on. But as a political project, it may be helpful instead to conceptualize the human right to housing as a bundle of rights—*the right to shelter*; *the right to a home*; and *the right to the city*—and consider them in comparison to the New York City we know today.

Taken in that order—shelter, home, city—these rights become more complex and challenging to implement, but each is ultimately essential to any conception of a holistic right to housing:

an order under which any loss of housing would be rare, short, and compassionately treated; in which one could just as easily stay where they are or move somewhere else, as needs and desires dictate over time; and in which people can collectively determine what around them must change and what should be preserved.

Since 1981, New York City has had perhaps the strongest right to shelter anywhere in the country. While this right is legally binding and enforceable, it is not secured by a specific law. Instead, it is the result of a consent decree based on a judicial interpretation of a clause in the New York State Constitution. This ruling came in the case of *Callahan v. Carey*. Robert Callahan was a homeless man who had been sleeping on the streets of the Lower East Side; Hugh Carey was the governor of New York State.

Callahan's lawyer, Robert Hayes, argued that the question boiled down to a single word in a clause added to the constitution in 1938: "The aid, care and support of the needy are public concerns and shall be provided by the state and by such of its subdivisions, and in such manner and by such means as the legislature may from time to time determine." That one word? "Shall." Not *may* be provided, if the state is able or so chooses, but *shall* be provided, regardless of political or financial exigencies. As Hayes told reporter Ian Frazier, "In our presentation before the judge, we simply argued that 'shall' means 'shall.'"[1]

Tragically, Robert Callahan died shortly before the judge's ruling, and he was never given the access to shelter his lawsuit ushered in. Litigants went on to sue the city many times thereafter to ensure this right to shelter was provided by the city, fully and fairly, to all who had nowhere else to go.[2]

More than two decades later, the right to shelter still stands, though it strains under the weight of worsening homelessness. There exists today a shelter archipelago sprawling unevenly across the city, some shelters easily perceptible and others nondescript.

Single adults are often shuffled into congregate shelters, considered by residents to be the least comfortable or safe environments. Some offer more privacy, while others are more like barracks. In fact, some of them *are* barracks—massive urban armories that once served as staging grounds for armed forces often deployed to put down strikes and riots.

Families with children must be sheltered under higher standards, which can look like partial or whole apartment buildings or hotels with private bedrooms and bathrooms but little in the way of kitchens. There is also a myriad of special-purpose shelters, including those specifically for people fleeing intimate partner violence—among the top proximate causes of homelessness in New York—for runaway homeless youth, and for those living with HIV/AIDS. In 2025, New York City opened the country's first shelter specifically for trans people, offering space for 150 occupants.[3] Altogether, in 2025, the city and its contractors maintain spaces for over 112,000 people—more shelter beds than the entire population of Boulder, Colorado.[4]

To access the right to shelter for more than a few days, applicants must demonstrate that they have no place else to go: no family or friends to stay with, and not enough money to pay for their own housing. They may be offered a one-way ticket out of the city if they have someone elsewhere to live with or somewhere else they would rather be.

Once someone is in the shelter system, the average stay lasts a little over a year.[5] Some shelter residents get fed up and leave on their own, often to return shortly thereafter, given the harsh reality of life on the streets. Some find placements in public housing or new private developments with set-asides for the formerly homeless. Most get out using a voucher that will help pay the cost of a private apartment.

Despite the remarkably high number of people in the shelter system—the population tripled in the first quarter of the twenty-first century[6]—most who seek shelter are turned away for allegedly failing to meet the city's criteria. Between 2017 and 2024, families with children were denied shelter 64 percent of the time; families without kids faced a 75 percent rejection rate.[7] This forced families to settle or scramble for whatever dangerous or substandard accommodation they could secure: an overcrowded apartment, an abusive relationship, a subway bench, a sidewalk. In New York City today, over 200,000 households live in overcrowded homes, doubled or tripled up with other families. A large but unverifiable number live informally in housing the city might classify as uninhabitable, including flood-prone basements or firetrap attics. Others engage in the practice casually known as "couch surfing," a euphemism that paints this physically and emotionally arduous existence as a pleasant day at the beach.

Taking all these populations together—those in formal shelters, those living in subways, parks, and streets, and those crammed precariously into unstable quarters—the Coalition for the Homeless estimates the city's true homeless population at 350,000 people.[8] Ironically—or perhaps causally—this is approximately the same number of millionaires in the city. To engage in a bit of vulgar Marxism: poverty exists because wealth exists, as wealth derives from the exploitation of labor and the state power to protect private property. In New York City, this manifests in a one-to-one relationship between the richest and the poorest. A representative sample of twenty-four New Yorkers—about the median number of homes in a New York City apartment building—would find one to be homeless, and one a millionaire. As the city becomes less and less affordable to the tenants in between, the number of both destitute and deep-pocketed New Yorkers continues to rise.

Given this litany of horrors, it is worth questioning whether, in fact, the right to shelter is even compatible with the right to housing—let alone foundational to it, as I suggested earlier. It is fairly common in New York City to hear that the right to shelter and the obscene quantities the city spends on its homeless services only reproduce homelessness and make permanent housing more distant.

From the right, this sentiment is usually paired with a behavioralist attitude, which views homelessness as a consequence of individual choices rather than the structural outcome of low wages, meager welfare, and overpriced housing, and thus frames shelters and other services as incentives to homelessness. This is absurd and insulting on a number of levels, including the fact that the very behaviors and conditions many assume cause homelessness (such as substance abuse and mental illness) are often instead consequences of or coping mechanisms for homelessness, and the rather paltry evidence that any meaningful subset of tenants—let alone a majority of those who wind up in shelter—voluntarily gives up stable housing for the "comforts" and "privileges" of being homeless.

But from the left, critics rightly point to the money spent on shelters that could be spent instead on permanent housing and see the sporadic scandals that erupt over embezzlement and misappropriation of funds passing through the homeless system as evidence of a booming shelter-industrial complex. More profoundly, some wonder if having the right to shelter papers over the severity of the permanent housing crisis and excuses the city from enacting a true right to housing. If there were no right to shelter, perhaps we could force the city to deal with mass homelessness through mass housing, rather than through mass shelter.

A few years ago, my friend Eric Goldfischer told me about a conversation he had with the late legendary homeless organizer Nikita Price. Eric was doing participatory action research with Picture the Homeless, an organization of currently and formerly homeless New Yorkers organizing for radical solutions to the private, commodified systems of housing and land ownership. He became especially close with Nikita, and when they weren't talking about family or baseball, they often found themselves in long political and philosophical conversations. In one such debate, Eric held the position that as long as the city maintained its massive shelter system, there would always be mass homelessness. One enabled the other and created powerful incentives toward state inertia and inaction.

Nikita, though he had countless critiques of the shelter system, insisted that even in a city with an ironclad right to housing, shit would still happen: interpersonal conflicts, weather emergencies, fires, and more. People will always need a place to get away, so the point of the system should be to get them back where they want to be with as much care and as little trauma as possible.

Eric had a strong point about how the right to shelter operates now, but Nikita's vision of a better but never calamity-proof future rings true to me. The city we seek to create can't possibly be one in which nothing ever goes wrong but must instead be a place that is ready to care for any of us when the worst happens. A right to shelter should be evidence that a society cares about those in the grip of calamity, and not an excuse not to care more. It must be a component of a right to housing and never a substitute for it.

The link between the right to shelter and the right to a home can be broached through an approach known as "housing first." Rather than insisting that people experiencing homelessness go through a litany of tests to prove their poverty, or enter into medical, psychological, or behavioral treatment programs to prove that they are "housing ready," the housing first model aims to get people into a safe and stable home as quickly as possible, and then it offers social and medical supports on a voluntary and ongoing basis thereafter. As a report commissioned by the Finnish government explained, "In the Housing First model, a dwelling is not a reward that a homeless person receives once their life is back on track. Instead, a dwelling is the foundation on which the rest of life is put back together."[9]

Finland operates the world's best known and most developed housing first system. Though the operations look somewhat different from city to city within the country, the overall approach is to get people into homes—sometimes vacant apartments scattered across apartment complexes, sometimes hostels and hotels converted into permanent housing—give them money to pay the rent, and bring in medical and social workers to offer their services. Largely as a result of this program, Finland reduced its homeless population by two-thirds between 1987 and 2017, leaving only the category of "staying with friends or family" relatively stable over time.[10]

It feels strange to say this, given the depths of New York City's homelessness crisis, but our city has already instituted a remarkably successful housing first plan. Beginning in 2011, the federal and city governments created a program of rental assistance vouchers and social supports for homeless military veterans. It put people directly into housing and offered them the physical and mental health services they needed. As a result, veteran homelessness dropped 90 percent, to what the government classifies as "functional zero" veteran homelessness.[11]

In a very large city, it is understandable to pilot an ambitious program like this on a subset of the population in order to ensure that the new system works. But once the pilot proves successful, it is unconscionable not to expand it to the more than 100,000 suffering through the system we have. And yet, New York City did not.

Perhaps it is unsurprising, then, that Finland, the country with the most advanced housing first approach to homelessness, also guarantees a right to housing in its national constitution. Housing first, according to the report referenced earlier, advances "the principle where a person does not have to first change their life around in order to earn the basic right to housing." If housing is truly to be understood as a human right, the only conditioning factor is humanity itself.

When most people think of a right to housing, they are conceiving of a right to a home—a city, nation, or world where no one is pushed into homelessness, and where no one is evicted because of tenant poverty or landlord avarice.

A right to a home means ensuring there is always enough housing for everyone, regardless of market conditions. It is not a right to real estate, or an entitlement to for-profit homeownership—a recipe for the kind of "predatory inclusion" Keeanga-Yamahtta Taylor warns against[12]—nor is it a promise of detached single-family homes on large lots for every resident—a program that would produce a sprawling mess. Rather it is a promise that plentiful, affordable, safe, and decent housing will always be accessible to all who need it.

There would be homes big enough for intergenerational families, of birth and of choice, and homes small enough for singles who prefer to live on their own. Buildings and apartments could be reconfigured across their users' lifecycles, as in the postwar Dutch Stichting Architecten Research model or the Japanese Metabolist movement, which imagined convertible buildings whose rooms would expand and contract, subdivide and combine, based on the household's or population's changing needs over time.[13] Alternatively, or additionally, cities could plan and build according to our present and predicted needs such that anyone could easily move into housing that better suits them at any given time.

With a right to a home, housing and neighborhoods would be designed to support children and the elderly. As the Viennese feminist planner Eva Kail has demonstrated throughout her career, projects, neighborhoods, and cities designed around the expressed desires of women, children, and the elderly are safer and more pleasant environments for all.[14] This is not only because, God willing, all of us will be both children and seniors at different points in our lifetime, but because everyone benefits from integrating healthcare with housing, creating balanced landscapes that offer both sunshine and shade, designing spaces to store strollers and scooters as well as grocery carts and bicycles, establishing safe passageways for pedestrians and combating autocentric transportation planning, and setting spaces aside for children and adults to relax, play, congregate, and seek solitude.

There must also be supportive housing that offers social and medical services alongside housing provision. Such housing exists in New York and many other cities today, but it is in too short supply, and—particularly when it is designed for the indigent—can slip into a carceral quality that undermines its capacity to deliver care. As groups like Supportive Housing Organized Tenants (SHOUT) insist, residents must be protected by the full battery of rights and protections afforded to every other tenant and not treated as a special and subordinate class.

In its best manifestations, supportive housing disrupts the dichotomy between housing and healthcare and instead offers the kinds of medical, psychological, and social services people need right where they live. Rather than forcing those who dwell there to accept these services, regardless of their own self-conception or self-determination, it offers services upon the residents' request, not at the providers' demand.

Perhaps most consequentially, if the right to a home is made real, then housing must be affordable to all, through some combination of resident contribution and public subsidy. If this sounds like I'm saying all housing would be public housing, it's because I am—and in fact, I am saying that in some ways, all housing is *already* public housing, or perhaps more precisely a public-private partnership.

David Madden and Peter Marcuse persuasively argue in their book *In Defense of Housing* that there is what we label as public housing—housing built, owned, and operated by a public authority; there is what we label subsidized housing—housing built by private entities but offered at a lower cost because of direct public spending; and there is what we call private housing, which nonetheless benefits from direct and indirect public subsidy through tax incentives or all-out tax exemptions, as well as through the array of public infrastructures that makes even the conception of private development on a site possible. None of it happens without public investment, and therefore none of it is purely private.

Perhaps more uncomfortably for leftists, under capitalism, even our public goods are linked to private investment, whether that comes through the bonds used to finance the construction of American public housing and other public infrastructure, or, less directly, the corporate tax revenue used to maintain government spending. In a city with a right to a home, this public dependency must be made explicit, rather than stigmatized for the poor and suppressed for the rich.

I am sometimes queasy about describing a better future in which housing is affordable to all, rich or poor, because in a better future, no one should be poor and no one should be rich—or rather everyone should enjoy the comforts and privileges the rich currently enjoy, and no one should be as wealthy as the billionaire class. But there is strong evidence to show that cities with expansive and well-functioning social housing systems also have less inequality. This manifests both in economic terms of incomes and wealth and in spatial terms of segregation and exclusion.[15]

And yet, an egalitarian housing movement can never be effective without a strong labor movement, as it will never on its own have the means to sufficiently discipline capital or to command the wages needed to match housing expenses. Subsidizing housing for low-wage workers is an essential component of a left housing program, but in isolation it can also serve as an indirect subsidy to low-wage employers, and thus an excuse for exploitation. What housing advocates might call "deeply affordable housing" (meaning housing at reduced cost for people earning extremely low incomes) labor organizers might characterize as public support for unconscionably low wages and structural underemployment. Housing unaffordability is as much a problem of low wages as it is high rents and sales prices, meaning that whether or not we consider tenants to be a class in itself (let alone for itself), the housing struggle is and will always be an inseparable element of the class struggle.

The general left conception of a right to a home demands that some level of the state—or, for anarchists and state-skeptics, other democratic and accountable social formations—must be primarily responsible for ensuring the provision of universally affordable housing. It may come directly from the state, in the case of government-built housing, or it may come from working-class institutions imbricated with state systems, such as land trusts, labor unions, political party offshoots, or social collectives of likeminded neighbors. Either way, homes would be decoupled from the private market, and the system would prioritize the right to a home over anyone's ability to profit from exploiting this universal human need.

There is, however, an increasingly popular countervailing model that emphasizes private supply over public provision and locates the root of the housing crisis in overly strict zoning codes. This orientation has left and right variations, with the former (leftists) viewing zoning regulations as a means for the landowners' lobby to artificially constrain the housing supply in order to tighten the market and drive-up prices, and the latter (rightists) viewing zoning regulations as an unjustifiable government overreach into private property rights.

Left arguments for loosening or abolishing zoning implicitly point to the political aspects of "full housing," along the lines of Polish economist Michal Kalecki's classic 1943 work on the "Political Aspects of Full Employment."[16] In that influential essay, Kalecki showed that establishing full employment (through intensive government action as well as private provision) strips capitalists of their power to discipline labor, because workers will be emboldened to risk being fired in full confidence that they will easily find work elsewhere. This, Kalecki argued, is the primary reason full employment engenders such intense opposition from business owners, who otherwise pride themselves on being self-described "job creators."

In a parallel manner, [illegible] critics of zoning regulations argue that [illegible] combination of government and pri[illegible]s were allowed to build homes for al[illegible]rds could not so readily discipline tenan[illegible] the fear of arbitrary rent hikes and the specter of homelessness. Tenants could more easily challenge their landlords' rent setting abilities or failure to maintain their buildings if they had the power to walk out and easily find another home.

The debate on the left, then, might most productively center on whether, in the absence of zoning constraints, private developers would actually build enough supply to create homes for all—and if they did, whether they would continue to rent them out to increasingly assertive and organized tenants. Kalecki's analysis would suggest not, just as private employers will never on their own accord achieve or maintain full employment.

This is not to defend the indefensible status quo of American land use law, but rather to clarify that no matter how we rewrite our zoning codes, there will have to be a strong role for the state, not only to keep capitalists from maintaining tight housing markets, but to build the homes for-profit developers won't—be that low-cost apartments or, in some markets, simply any housing at all.

I suspect some in my audience may be craving a Yes in My Backyard (YIMBY) takedown here. I have been notedly critical of this political framing, whose acronymic imprecision prompts infinite queries. (Yes to anything? What are the spatial boundaries of "my backyard," if the movement seeks more everywhere? Does the reference to backyards suggest that YIMBYism is perhaps a reasonable response to suburban reactionaries, rather than a program designed for already dense cities, where nonmetaphorical backyards are hard to come by?)

But I would like to put aside these differences and instead point to the broiling temperature of the argument over land use, zoning, and development. The urgency of these debates over how best to achieve the right to a home underscores how far we are from having such a right in New York City or elsewhere in the United States and much of the world.

As discussed earlier, homelessness is an epidemic. Among the housed, nearly half of US renters are rent burdened, or paying more than 30 percent of their income toward rent each month, and in many places there is little available that would cost less than the homes they already have but can barely afford. Rents and sales prices have skyrocketed since the COVID pandemic began, and they were already inflated to begin with. Low-income New Yorkers are being squeezed out of central neighborhoods and into longer and longer commutes or are being pushed out of the city and state altogether.

According to the Fiscal Policy Institute, the groups exiting New York State at the highest rate are households earning less than $104,000, and particularly those earning between $32,000 and $65,000.[17] Those making the most are leaving at the lowest rate, despite the claims that New York's tax and regulatory regimes are driving away the state's highest earners and highest individual taxpayers. Thirty-six percent of those exiting the state say they are doing so in pursuit of more affordable housing, doubling the proportion leaving for that reason before COVID. The vast majority of those leaving New York State—90 percent—are departing from New York City.[18]

As both a cause and a consequence of all these factors, real estate capital maintains excessive power over our governments, and over our lives. This makes it incredibly challenging to achieve an actionable right to a home: it is hard to have a right to something that is someone else's business, especially when that business is one of the most valuable and politically potent forces in many cities—and, if you include homeownership as a promise of wealth building, in the country as a whole. In the system we have today, the right to profit from housing supersedes the right to a home.

That prioritization has produced a familiar form of political pathology we can readily recognize across jurisdictions. Landlords and developers use their concentrated power to weaken existing rights and protections, forestall tenants' political advances, and control the means of housing production such that the kinds of housing people need most are delivered minimally, if at all. Those who own their home privately (that is, not as part of a shared equity model of cooperative ownership) become extremely protective of their home's exchange value, and, instead of arguing for a more generalized distribution of social benefits, often embrace the most exclusionary and revanchist forms of homeowner politics. City politics become similarly sociopathic as the city becomes dependent on rising property tax revenue (as well as income taxes from rich people and corporate tax revenue from big businesses), creating a sizable barrier to confronting the problems of wealth hoarding and unaffordable housing.

For all of these reasons, we need a yet-greater political horizon, captured by the concept and slogan of "the right to the city." While difficult to condense into a succinct definition, the right to the city encompasses the universal right to benefit from all that cities uniquely offer and the collective right of urban dwellers to determine their cities' trajectories. It was first enumerated by the French polymath Henri Lefebvre in his 1968 essay *Le droit à la ville*.

Reading Lefebvre in the original French is likely challenging, but in translation his work presents as equally illuminating and loopy. The right to the city is tantalizing but it is not exactly self-evident. In one helpful—if still challenging—passage, Lefebvre defines and contextualizes the right to the city alongside the "right to work, to training and education, to health, housing, leisure, to life," and frames them as part of the triumph of "use value" over "exchange value," in classically Marxist terms—in other words, a right that can only be won through the total transformation of society.

"Among these rights in the making," he continues,

> features the *right to the city* (not to the ancient city, but to urban life, to renewed centrality, to places of encounter and exchange, to life rhythms and time uses, enabling the full and complete *usage* of these moments and places, etc.). The proclamation and realization of urban life as the rule of use (of exchange and encounter disengaged from exchange value) insist on the mastery of the economic (of exchange value, the market, and commodities) and consequently is inscribed within the perspectives of the revolution under the hegemony of the working class.[19]

When Lefebvre wrote these words, revolution was imminent. In May 1968, workers and students were striking, rioting, striking again, and rebelling against the system in every way possible. Beneath the paving stones, the Situationists promised, lay the beach. Lefebvere was helping the world understand what could come next, how new forms of socialism could deliver novel and previously unenumerated rights. France, of course, went a different route, as did much of the world in the 1970s, when we all learned a new word to explain the rightward counterrevolution: "neoliberalism."[20]

In recent years, however, the right to the city has returned to prominence as a means to pry open our political imaginations. Around the world, left social movements have fought to establish the right to the city in metropolitan and national constitutions. New processes were devised to popularize urban politics and incorporate worker, peasant, tenant, and transit-rider movements into contentious new planning and budgeting methods. In the US, following the 2008 financial crisis (a crisis of housing speculation, let us not forget), the right to the city took off as a framework to combat financialization and expand community ownership.

But despite its avid following in corners of the left, the concept can still prove baffling to people when they first encounter it. We are so divorced from its revolutionary origins, and it sounds so unlike any other kinds of rights we might be used to conceptualizing. In practical terms, it seems to present a frustratingly frictionless vision of urban space. Anyone used to the passionate fights that often arise not just across but *within* class lines over the use of ostensibly public spaces—be they lanes of streets to be dedicated to cars, bikes, or pedestrians, parks to be shared by children and adults with very different ideas of what constitutes leisure and decorum, or publicly owned vacant lots to be reimagined and redeveloped—understands that "the community" shares no singular will.

It is not just neophytes who find the concept of the right to the city befuddling—it continues to challenge scholars of this framework, too. Geographer Kafui Attoh, for example, asks, in the title of an article, "What Kind of Right Is the Right to the City?" To begin to answer this question, he offers such possibilities as "a socio-economic right or a liberty right, a legal right or a moral right, a prima facie right or an absolute right," before finally asking, "If it is simultaneously all of these rights, are such rights commensurable?"[21]

Along analogous lines, the documentarian Kelly Anderson titled a similar inquiry "Whose Right, to What City?" In that article, she asks particularly, "Who adjudicates it? Why does one group's right to the city matter more than another's? Is it just a matter of who has been here longer, or is something more fundamental at stake?"[22] In an even more challenging register, geographer Antonis Vradis asks if, by aiming for the city, we might be missing the point. This, he posits, reflects contemporary movements' "exodus through scale," or retreat from ambitious aims down to a more modest localism (or municipalism, as the case may be).[23]

All these are fair critiques, and perhaps they help explain why I have not referred to the right to the city in my own professional or political work all that often. But tacked to the wall beside my desk in the closet I use as a home office is a purple poster, designed by Josh MacPhee in tribute to the geographer David Harvey and distributed at a conference held at the City of New York's Center for Place, Culture and

Politics. The poster displays in its top-left corner a view of Midtown Manhattan, similar to the view from Harvey's perch at the CUNY Graduate Center. Then, in seven easy steps, we see instructions for how to fold the image into a paper airplane, take it in one's hand, and glide it into the future. Below the paper airplane is a quote from Harvey's book *Rebel Cities: From the Right to the City to the Urban Revolution*: "All those whose labors are engaged in producing and reproducing the city have a collective right not only to that which they produce, but also to decide what kind of urbanism is to be produced where, and how."

For me, that's it. That is why the right to the city matters, confounding though it may be. It puts an urban labor theory of value into the language of political and moral rights. The city, says Harvey (by way of Lefebvre), is the product of incalculably immense accretions of collective labor, some of it paid and some of it unpaid. Under capitalism, both the city we produce and the process to determine its future course are alienated from us by those who own its component parts. Our physical, cultural, and socially reproductive labor makes the city what it is, and every month we are forced to pay back a share of our earnings in exchange for our ability to enjoy any part in it.

In her work on gentrification and resistance in India, geographer Ipsita Chatterjee has developed the deepest parallel between the extraction of value from people's labor in commodity production, on the one hand, and the extraction of value from people's labor in spatial production on the other. ("Spatial production" is another somewhat challenging phrase offered to us by Lefebvre through his book *The Production of Space*. It refers to the inherently collective process of designing, developing, and embedding meaning in physical spaces.) In her book *Displacement, Revolution, and the New Urban Condition*, Chatterjee first demonstrates that labor—paid and unpaid, individual and collective—occurs not just on the shop floor but also in working-class people's homes, blocks, neighborhoods, and cities. Not only are people forced to take work home with them, but they devote additional labor to building up and sustaining their surroundings. They maintain their homes, they care for and educate themselves and others, they work to create and run social and political institutions, and they develop cultural practices (food, film, music, murals, vernacular architectures) that express their unique relationships to particular spaces and places. All of this takes a tremendous amount of effort, time, thought, and planning—in other words, labor.

If space is socially produced through labor, Chatterjee continues, then urban "displacement is as much 'estranged labor' as it is 'estranged spaces,'" defined as "a deprivation from the right to produce space and right to place-making."[24] Gentrification is not only a question of rising rents in working-class neighborhoods but exploitation in the classical sense. The same analytical tools that enable us to understand the process of estranged labor in the workplace can illuminate the process of estranged space in the neighborhood, and the same socialist imperative to confront and transform the alienation of labor at work can animate the spirit of an anti-gentrification politics. Establishing the right to the city would mean abolishing this form of exploitation and democratizing the housing and planning systems, such that the monopoly power of real estate capital is challenged and ultimately overturned.

When we combine the right to the city with the right to a home and the right to shelter, we might consider the right to the city as the means to democratically establish the systems to provide for the other two rights. In other words, a right to the city includes the collective right to a democratic and universal housing system.

In a piece for the magazine *Topos* a few years back, titled "Their Right to the City, and Ours," I argued that in the capitalist city as we know it today, the rich essentially have the right to the city already.[25] Through their ability to buy land and property, and through their outsized ability to shape city politics, the rich could very well claim that they have already secured the right to dictate the city's course and the particulars of its preservation and development. The right to the city is a fight to reverse this inequity, and to claim these powers for a much broader—if not always ideologically aligned—constituency.

This, then, is the fight for housing as a human right: a fight for the right to the city, the right to a home, and the right to shelter. They are nested rights, each constitutive of the others. It would be hard to say we have a right to a home if we do not have a right to shelter should disaster strike. It is equally hard to say that one has the right to the city without the right to a home within it. Without one, the others collapse. We New Yorkers have never known a city with all three, but that is what we must aspire to.

It may be impossible, however, to dive directly into a fight so large. And so instead, we struggle at the most local of levels—the sites of our bodies and our homes—for a higher degree of control over our housing. This is the core of tenant organizing, a practice New York City has honed over hundreds of years of struggle.

I was a tenant organizer for a few years because I thought it was the most important thing anyone who cared about New York could do. I organized tenant unions at the building level and tried to scale up the struggle by matching renters facing the same problems across the city and developing campaigns for policies that addressed those issues at their root.

It turned out I was not very good at it. Being an organizer requires a kind of charismatic confidence and infectious optimism that I could summon periodically but never sustain. I struggled to weigh the competing needs of particular buildings, which included both fights with landlords and conflicts among tenants, and of statewide campaigns, which required a high degree of unity and discipline. Often I felt like I was manipulating people when I tried to get them more involved in our organization. While I ultimately believed that we would win, in the abstract or in the future, I was never quite sure about the particulars in the present. The stakes felt as high as the barriers. These were the years of Republican majorities (numerical or maneuvered) in the State Senate and billionaire Bloomberg's third term as mayor, and I could not figure out how to build enough tenant power to overcome these political impediments.

At the same time, I was finding my voice as a writer and honing my skills as a researcher, and I concluded that I could do more for the movement as a decent author than as an inept organizer. I gave my notice, quit the job, attempted to write a never-completed book with the late great Peter Kwong, taught as an adjunct professor, eventually sought a PhD, and then found work as a researcher supporting New York's tenant and homeless movement. But in my time as an organizer, I learned a great deal about how the movement builds on contemporary and historical victories toward something like a human right to housing.

There are typically four components to this program, none of them unique to New York City: rental assistance, rent regulation, social housing conversions, and social housing development. Together they form a sideways approach to the right to housing, delivering a *de facto* rather than *de jure* answer to the question of how to secure this right for all.

Although this program can take the language and form of law—which can quickly turn dry, technocratic, and utterly insufficient to the task at hand—the separate components are also inherently dependent on ongoing struggle and so should not be reduced to the realm of pure policy. Not only could none of these components be achieved without dogged organizing and mobilizing, but neither could they be sustained or expanded. The model, therefore, is not policy as a substitute for organizing, but rather a feedback loop between organizing and policy that deepens and amplifies both: organizing to build power and make demands, new policies to protect and spark more organizing, more policy wins to follow, more organizing as a result, and on and on. As Francis

Fox Piven and Richard Cloward have demonstrated, this interaction has ebbed and flowed across US history, developing into a repertoire of struggle and governance that elides any easy distinction between policy and politics.[26]

Rental assistance may seem like a strange place for a leftist to start as it—combined with lifting land use restrictions—is the preferred housing policy approach for conservative (which is to say, mainstream) economists and centrist politicians. But though leftists may rightly look askance at rental assistance, we cannot look away entirely.

In the US context, rental assistance comes in two primary forms: tenant-based and project-based subsidies. As the names suggest, tenant-based assistance is attached to a qualifying renter, who can use it in whatever form of housing they choose within the appropriate geographic and cost parameters. (In other words, a State of New York–funded tenant-based housing voucher can't be used in Connecticut, any more than a federally funded US voucher can be used in Canada, nor can a voucher be used to rent a mansion or a luxury penthouse.) These demand-side vouchers impose two ceilings: an income cap on eligible tenants, usually pegged to "area median income," and a price cap on eligible apartments, usually pegged to a percentage of an area's typical rent. Area median income and local "fair market rents" are both calculated by statisticians in a shrinking federal Department of Housing and Urban Development, and both produce a strange and—for many tenants—inaccurate picture of local economic and housing conditions.

In a tenant-based voucher system, the renter pays a portion of their income toward rent and the sponsoring government agency pays the balance between the tenant's contribution and the home's full cost. As I write this in summer 2025, the tenant's contribution is generally pegged to 30 per cent of their income. I put that time stamp here because the Trump administration—a global symbol of landlord power—has sought to raise the threshold to 35 percent, while the Eric Adams administration is raising the standard to 40 per cent for certain recipients of city-controlled vouchers. As we push back against attempts to raise tenants' contribution level, it is worth remembering that 30 percent is *already* inflated from the previous standard, 25 percent of income, which was the norm until the Reagan administration.[27]

In contrast to tenant-based (or demand-side) vouchers, project-based subsidies (confusingly also called vouchers) are attached to particular buildings or apartments and remain in place from one qualifying tenancy to the next, unless and until the subsidies expire. These supply-side vouchers are usually part of a package of direct and indirect dollars and incentives that go into building new affordable housing, converting for-profit housing into nonprofit alternatives, or converting housing from one subsidy program to another. Residents usually qualify to live in the housing based on the same income criteria as a tenant-based voucher. These supply-side subsidies are generally preferred in countries and cities with strong social housing systems. The American system, however, tends to favor tenant-based subsidies, both in terms of budgets and discourse, because the tenant-based voucher stresses individual household choice and sub-national geographic mobility—two cornerstones of the ideology that makes neoliberalism appear as "common sense."

There are generally three strong left arguments against supporting these kinds of programs.

The first is that rental assistance is the government's way of paying the building owners we're otherwise fighting against. Sometimes these are social-sector owners, but more often they are the same profit-seeking landlords whose business model we might otherwise seek to abolish. The system could be reconfigured as a direct state payment to tenants, rather than building owners, but still—the money would end up in the landlord's pockets, and while the process might be more empowering to the renter, the effect would be much the same. Tenant-based vouchers may make housing more affordable to those lucky enough to secure them, but they do not fundamentally alter the balance of power between tenants and landlords. In fact, a voucher-holding tenant often has a harder time going on rent strike than a cash-paying tenant.

Second, because of the rent caps on vouchers—which are necessary to prevent landlords from charging truly obscene rents to the government—as well as the tight housing markets for homes under that threshold and the poor quality of much of the private low-rent housing stock, voucher holders may end up settling for housing they would otherwise reject if they had more choices (which is to say more money). While tenant-based vouchers are premised on the idea of "moving to opportunity," or getting out of low-income and racialized enclaves and moving to richer areas with better-funded school systems and other public services, they do not always function this way. In New York City, public housing—which was built unevenly but expansively across the city's five boroughs—is today better integrated at the neighborhood level than housing vouchers, which tend to be concentrated in just a few very low-income areas.[28] (To be clear, this comparison does not hold up at the building level, where New York City public housing may be more diverse than popular imagination dictates but remains super-majority low-income and about 90 percent Black and Latino.[29])

Third, there is a historical argument. The right wing in the US has long preferred tenant subsidies to building public housing. In 1973, President Nixon imposed a moratorium on new federally funded public housing construction and initiated a shift in federal funding to vouchers. This move had the combined effect of further destabilizing public housing, which was always underfunded, while normalizing yet another transfer of wealth from the public coffers to private landlords and developers. And yet, even these vouchers were never properly funded, leaving four out of five eligible households unaided or languishing on long waiting lists.[30] From this perspective, America's de facto solution to the housing unaffordability crisis is a cruel joke: a broken promise premised on the government's unwillingness to simply house the public.

These arguments are not wrong, particularly when we are talking about tenant-based vouchers. They *are* a payment to landlords, and often the same ones we're organizing against. But there are other government payments to capitalists that the left does not generally subject to the same degree of stigma. We do not often hear left formations in the United States decrying food vouchers (aka food stamps or food assistance programs) as subsidies to private grocers that disincentivize the public provision of food as a human right. Perhaps this is because we do not often contrast private grocery stores with underfunded public ones, as we do for housing, but still, the discrepancy is instructive.

There is also the issue of urgency. With over 100,000 people in New York City homeless shelters alone, there is a need for housing *now*. Efforts to prevent eviction and keep rents low will help those numbers from swelling further; building new social housing will help people when the developments are up and running; but neither will immediately get people out of desperate and often dangerous conditions and into safe and permanent housing. Left critics of the shelter-industrial complex rightly point out that on a month-by-month basis, it would be significantly cheaper to house a person in need in a typical apartment than to pay for the full cost of shelter. One cannot make this case and then turn against rental assistance, as "housing a person in need in a typical apartment" means, essentially, offering them rental assistance.

This voucher-paid housing need not be privately owned. Even in decommodified housing, operating costs often exceed what many residents can afford. This is in large part because, barring a greater social transformation, the inputs to decommodified housing—from the land on which it is built to the labor that constructs and maintains it to the materials that make up its foundations to the energy that keeps it going—all maintain their commodity status. A "cost rent" system, in which the charge to tenants is pegged to what it costs to maintain a building, would be far preferable to allowing whatever the market will bear, but it will still produce rents beyond many households' budgets.[31]

Poverty, unemployment, underemployment, and insufficient wages are far from fringe conditions in New York City, or elsewhere. The term "extremely low-income" used in housing policy circles might conjure a small fraction of the population, but in New York City this lowest-earning category represents one in four renters. In fact, most New York City households (including both renters and owners across the five boroughs) qualify as "low-income" according to official statistics. In the Bronx, over three-quarters of households fall below this threshold.[32] For this reason, even some of the left's preferred housing models, including those like community land trusts that are conceptualized as an alternative to direct government provision, often *still* rely on vouchers in order to be affordable.

Vouchers themselves are agnostic to housing typologies. They can be—and indeed *usually* are today—used to get low-income tenants into private, for-profit, otherwise market-rate housing. This is no way to resolve the housing crisis. But they can also be—and indeed *already* are—used in combination with rent control and social housing. In fact, the only way to make real the promise of "choice" for voucher holders would be to seriously scale up the social housing sector, which welcomes rather than discriminates against tenants paying for housing with public assistance, and offers voucher-paying tenants a wider variety of neighborhoods and housing typologies to select from or move between at different stages of life.

While vouchers have come to normalize government support for private profits, voucher systems also normalize the concept of socializing housing prices—that is, spreading the cost of housing across all of society via taxes and budgeting. The problem is that federal and local governments have normalized *this* means of socializing housing prices while stigmatizing public housing. As we reach toward achieving a human right to housing, the left does not have to do the opposite and stigmatize vouchers while celebrating public housing. We can, in fact, promote both at the same time as we seek to impose universal regulations on all private housing (whether or not vouchers are present) and build up social housing models that can use vouchers as one of many means to lower rents.

In the meantime, however, the politics can be extremely tricky to navigate. Coalitions for stronger rental assistance invariably include not only homeless and low-income tenant organizing groups, who see rental assistance as an immediate form of harm reduction and a long-term strategy of state support for housing, but also the landlords and developers who immediately and directly benefit from vouchers—under the current order at least—as well as politicians who are often at odds with the left.

Allow me a brief digression to share a personal experience with this "strange bedfellows" phenomenon. Think back to the heady days of "Build Back Better," when the early Biden administration was pushing a bill to massively expand environmental and social spending on multiple fronts. In those times, before the entire project came to a crushing defeat, centrist Democrats in high places seemed to be scared enough of the Sanders-aligned left to back big parts of its domestic agenda. With rumor of Alexandria Ocasio-Cortez mulling a run for US Senate, suddenly Chuck Schumer—elevated to the position of Senate majority leader—was joining Zoom calls with tenant organizations and pushing bills that would refund public housing to the tune of $170 billion and "universalize" vouchers (or actually fund them to the level needed to cover everyone who qualifies for them).

The biggest backer of the voucher component of this program was Bronx congressmember Ritchie Torres, who was far to my right on some issues. I clearly remember attending a press conference in the parking lot of Torres's Bronx district office on August 10, 2021, where he was extolling the virtues of expanding rental assistance to all who need it. I talked there with a colleague who specializes in budget analysis, who told me he found everything about this bill plausible except the idea that the US government would spend billions more on any program that benefits the poor—even if it also benefitted landlords. At some point—I believe during Bronx Borough President Vanessa Gibson's remarks—the assembled press started muttering among themselves, and when it came time for questions, they all just packed up and left. It turned out that as we were assembling, then-Governor Andrew Cuomo announced that he was resigning from office in recognition of a massive sexual harassment and bullying scandal. So much for making the news.

There was, however, a picture taken by a *New York Times* photographer showing Torres at the podium, and me, slightly out of focus, standing directly behind him. I know this not because the *Times* ran a story on our demand for robust rental assistance; I know this because three years later, on June 5, 2024, the *Times* ran a story headlined "Israel Secretly Targets U.S. Lawmakers with Influence Campaign on Gaza War."[33] Below were two photographs of this campaign's top targets. On the right was a portrait of Brooklyn Democrat and Congressional Majority Leader Hakeem Jeffries, standing boldly in profile in front of a solid black background. On the left was a picture of Torres, speaking confidently into a microphone, with me standing right behind him. I was their shadowy Jew looming behind the Afro-Latino Democrat. Goodbye, Soros; hello, Stein! All day I kept zooming in on that photo because I couldn't believe my eyes, only to see my own eyes glaring back at me.

By that point, Build Back Better was long dead, killed by two conservative Democrats who likely represented the will of several more, and we had proceeded into a much grimmer phase of Bidenism. The echo from three years prior seemed to have come from another world entirely, but it was a reminder of the uncomfortable coalitions in store for leftists fighting for money for tenants, money we knew would ultimately redound to their landlords.

At another press conference on voucher universalization I remember attending during that time, a reporter asked Congressman Torres whether landlords would raise the rents on voucher-olding tenants since they knew the government would be forced to pick up the tab. "No," Torres responded, seemingly baffled by the proposition. "They can't do that under rent stabilization." From Torres's district's perspective this made perfect sense. Nearly all the tenants using Section 8 vouchers were doing so in buildings subject to rent stabilization or some other regulatory framework. But across the country—even across the city—this is not necessarily the norm. When asked in a follow-up if he supported national rent control, Torres's nonchalant one-word answer was: "Sure!"

The fact that a Bronx Congressman so casually endorsed national rent control, a policy largely outside the national party's comfort zone, demonstrates the deep support these laws hold in New York City. Thanks to nonstop organizing and mass tenant action, New York has had some form of rent stabilization for over 100 years. Since 2019, when the tenant movement achieved a historic victory with the state's Housing Stability and Tenant Protection Act, the current form of rent stabilization is stronger than it has been for decades—and in some ways, stronger than ever before. Although the program's strictness has ebbed and flowed through its different iterations, some legislated by the city and others by the state, it remains a core part of the city's housing system for three primary reasons: it is relatively simple, it has a mass base, and it works.

It might seem strange to call New York's rent stabilization and rent control systems simple, given that they involve a bevy of particular and changing rights on topics ranging from rent setting to succession, but at their core is a basic principle: in a rough housing market, landlords should not be able to raise their rents arbitrarily, and tenants in good standing should be allowed to stay put. To a degree, the rest is details.

As of 2023, there were 960,700 rent-stabilized and 76,580 rent-controlled apartments in New York City. Taken together, these "rent-regulated" apartments comprise just under half the private rental stock. This is a massive constituency. It leans lower-income, more racially diverse, more immigrant, and more likely to include someone with a disability than either market-rate rentals or owner-occupied housing. But because it is not and has never been a means-tested or neighborhood-specific program, it is also hard to pigeonhole rent-stabilized tenants as any one particular type, or to write them off as an insignificant voting bloc.[34]

It is not a universal program, though we fight to make it so. For those covered, it has worked to keep rents much lower than comparable "market-rate" homes. Median rents for rent-stabilized apartments are 25 percent lower (or $500 per month less) than market-rate apartments, and far lower than the typical vacant market-rate apartment a tenant could move into today. But lower rents are just one reason why rent regulation is so popular in New York, and why preserving and expanding it must be a core element of our fight to secure a right to housing.[35]

As rent regulation reduces rents, it also enhances stability. Whereas a rightless renter cannot predict their costs from year to year, or even month to month in some cases, a rent-stabilized tenant knows that the landlord cannot raise their rent without some form of state sanction, be it the annual adjustment voted on by the public Rent Guidelines Board or a specialized state permission based on investments landlords may make. In this way, ironically, a rent-stabilized tenant shares something more in common with a typical homeowner than a market-rate renter: since the New Deal, most US homeowners have thirty-year fixed-rate mortgages, where the debtor expects to pay the bank the exact same amount every single month for decades on end. While rent-stabilized tenants know their rent may increase from year to year, they are assured it will not skyrocket arbitrarily due to housing market conditions.

In addition to predictable rents, rent stabilization denies landlords the dictatorial power to arbitrarily terminate a lease. A rent-stabilized lease guarantees the tenant the right to renew, as long as they have abided by the terms of the contract. In other words, the tenant has a right to remain, and the landlord cannot force them out due to prejudice, preference, or personality. Since 2017, this has been coupled with a right to counsel via free legal representation for low-income tenants facing eviction. (This right is subject to appropriations, however, and a double bind of underfunding for the program and underpay for the lawyers has left far too many tenants unprotected.) In recent years, the tenant movement has won increased stability for most market-rate tenants as well, with a "good cause" law passed in 2024 that gives such tenants a right to sue if their landlord denies them a lease renewal without cause or conditions that renewal on an exorbitant and unjustifiable rent increase.

The right to a lease coupled with the right to an attorney gives tenants a level of stability not commonly associated with renting in the broader United States, where being a tenant comes with unpredictable rent hikes and evictions. Renting without rent regulation and a right to counsel is inherently unstable. This—combined with entrenched class and race bigotry—has led many homeowners to associate tenancy itself with transience and communal disinterest. Not only is this prejudice unfair, but it blames the renter for their own inability to stay rooted in one place and get deeply involved in its social life and political culture before being forced to move. Rent stabilization, then, helps level the social hierarchy between renters and owners, offering residents an equal opportunity to form deep, long-term social and spatial ties and join together in civic and political projects.

Rent-regulated tenants are also more likely to assert their rights, without fear of any landlord punitively denying them a renewal lease. This may lead a tenant to speak up individually, or, more importantly, to organize with their fellow tenants and form a union. This kind of organizing has long been practiced in New York City and, as rent regulation gains popularity and wins in more and more cities and states, is becoming a larger part of the political culture around the country. This kind of organizing looks very different in different places, with some tenant unions behaving more like the Wobblies (that is, operating autonomously and waging constant battle against the landlord class, with the ultimate goal of expropriation) and others more like the AFL-CIO (that is, building durable institutions that seek to collectively bargain with landlords, with the ultimate goal of securing contractual rights). There is a growing debate over whether it might be possible and worthwhile to codify tenants' collective bargaining rights into law, and if so, in what form and at what scale. With or without such a codified system, the growth of the tenant union movement alongside the expansion of rent regulation demonstrates a feature of the system, not a fluke.

One aspect of rent regulation that is most dear to me often goes unmentioned in housing policy and movement discussions: the ability to disconnect housing prices from neighborhood changes, and particularly from public investments. In an unregulated rental market, when a neighborhood gets better, the prices go up. If the city invests in better schools, parks, transit, and infrastructure, if better supermarkets and athletic facilities open up nearby, and if neighboring building owners (be they private, nonprofit, or public entities) improve their holdings, tenants can reasonably expect their rent is going to rise—not necessarily because it became any more expensive for their landlord to maintain their building, or because their landlord made costly investments in their housing, but simply because someone else might now be willing to pay more to live in your newly upgraded neighborhood.

In a well-regulated rental market, all the same public and social investments can take place, but building owners are not able to capture the value and transmute it into higher rents. In most rent regulation systems, landlords can raise the rent a specified amount if they invest in their own buildings, but they cannot so easily capture the fruits of other people's labor based solely on market conditions. Because of this, rent-regulated tenants can more easily join in calls for public investment and neighborhood development than market-rate tenants because they know they—and even future generations of their family—will be able to stay and enjoy their improved surroundings without the fear that positive change will lead to gentrification and displacement. Universal rent control is therefore a necessary precondition for democratic planning.

Taking all these benefits together, we can see that while rent regulation may not decommodify housing as such, it powerfully lessens housing's commodity status. To unpack that claim, let me first explain why rent-stabilized housing remains a kind of commodity. It is bought and sold on the private market, and its exchange value fluctuates over time based on buyers' cyclical interests; it is backed by a bevy of mortgages, loans, and other financial products; and while the rate of rent adjustments is set annually through a political process, the apartments' base rents were originally set by developers and landlords according to market conditions.

But the commodity status of rent-stabilized housing is severely reduced by the regulatory framework, which limits rent increases and therefore suppresses property value inflation. Before the 2019 reforms, when it was much easier for landlords to raise rents and remove apartments from the system, speculation was rampant, and sales prices rose dramatically during real estate boom times. Since 2019, prices have fallen dramatically such that they are much more in-line with what the rents command, rather than what an investor might hope them to be after they leave the regulatory system. Banks are much less interested in letting landlords pursue cash-out refinancing and pull the equity from their buildings because lenders are not confident there will be a buyer on the other side to pick up the property for an elevated price. If rent-stabilized housing remains a commodity, it is a palpably cooler one than it used to be.

Most rent-stabilized landlords are doing just fine under this stricter system, even if they claim poverty and lobby to roll back tenants' legislative victory—so far with very limited success. But others bet big on the old system and its prospects for deregulation and limitless rent increases. They took out massive mortgages their current rent levels could not possibly sustain, and then, when the legislature took action to ban decontrol and limit rent hikes, they found themselves summarily screwed. In these cases, a predatory firm may now swoop in to pick off whatever profit they can from failing buildings, continuing to collect rent while investing less in repairs and maintenance. But another possibility remains, one that will be central to a future right to housing.

Instead of letting buildings bounce from buyer to buyer, we must instead pursue a program of "social housing conversions." Before describing exactly what I mean by that, let's start with the stirring but slippery language "social housing."

As of just a few years ago, I do not think I ever really used this term, or at least not when talking about this country. As with many in my milieu, though, it slipped into my lexicon following the release of a 2018 People's Policy Project report by Saoirse Gowan and Ryan Cooper titled *Social Housing in the United States*.

I can't say I was immediately onboard, but the clarifying work of my late mentor Tom Waters and my (thankfully very much alive) friend Oksana Mironova helped me see that rather than a pure binary between the social and the anti-social, there exists a vast and complex set of spectra along which we can chart historical, contemporary, and imaginary housing schemes. According to their matrix, published in early 2020, housing becomes more "social" when it is less commodified, more resident controlled, and—perhaps most complexly—promotes the greatest degree of social equality, by which they meant both vertically within a building (no more or less access or privileges depending on income or race) and horizontally across a city (no lesser quality or accessibility than their neighbors' housing).[36] To this, the sociologists Gianpaolo Baiocchi and Jacob Carlson add the criteria of greater decarbonization, arguing that in the context of already ruinous climate change, for housing to be social it must also be sustainable.[37]

Although debates rage about particular classifications, in the New York context, public housing, limited-equity cooperatives, community land trusts (CLTs), and mutual housing associations (MHAs) can all be modes of delivering social housing. Other housing types may qualify as well, but the strongest case can be made for these four.

Public housing consists of rentals owned and operated by government entities. Limited-equity cooperatives are buildings where residents own shares and cannot make much (or, in some cases, any) profit from the sale of their apartments. Community land trusts are nonprofit and democratically governed institutions that own land and, rather than selling plots outright, offer long-term leases at below-market rates. Mutual housing associations are a form of nonprofit ownership where tenants form a majority of the governing board and thus self-manage the housing without personally owning the property.

Taking all these forms together, roughly 9 percent of New York's housing stock qualifies as social housing. If that means that 91 percent falls somewhere on the "anti-social" side of the ledger, this can be dispiriting; but 9 percent of the largest city in the country is not a bad place to begin.

Returning to the idea of social housing conversions, we can see that a small but significant portion of the city's social housing stock was created by remaking buildings' ownership and governance models, rather than being purpose-built as social housing from the ground up. This model holds personal resonance because I have lived in such housing for the past five years, but it also holds special resonance for this moment, as some buildings decline due to speculative debts their regulated rents could never repay.

There are multiple means for and outcomes of such conversions. The city could foreclose on failing landlords and operate the buildings as municipal public housing, transfer the ownership to a CLT and an MHA, or offer the buildings to the residents as limited-equity cooperatives. Although the third model (tenant ownership through limited-equity cooperatives) has been the most prevalent in New York, the city has pursued all three of these paths. There are still brownstone buildings in neighborhoods like the

Upper West Side of Manhattan where landlords faced foreclosure and the city acquired and converted the town houses into public housing. It has happened before, and there is no legal or technical reason why it cannot happen again.

Most of the social housing conversions under this model take place in areas of landlord distress and even abandonment. The map of such conversions already in place in New York largely corresponds to areas with deep divestment in the 1970s and '80s, including the South Bronx, Washington Heights, Harlem, Hell's Kitchen, the Lower East Side, Williamsburg, and Central Brooklyn. Several of these areas have since gone through rounds of gentrification, making the existence and retention of public housing, limited-equity cooperatives, CLTs, and MHAs even more crucial.

Alternately, the city, state, or federal government could pass an "opportunity to purchase act," granting the local government and/or the tenants the right of first refusal whenever a qualified building goes up for sale. The residents could then have the choice of social housing model and operator, ranging from self-ownership (limited-equity cooperative) to public ownership to community control. While housing and community groups in New York City and state fight to enact versions of these laws here, Washington, DC, has a longer history of this kind of program. Since 1980, the District of Columbia has maintained a Tenant Opportunity to Purchase Act (TOPA) system, and in 2008 the city added a District Opportunity to Purchase Act (DOPA) component.

These rights-based programs have resulted in the transformation of thousands of for-profit rentals into limited-equity cooperatives. And even when the tenants opt not to purchase the building, it gives them a significant degree of bargaining rights with their future landlord at the point of sale, a time when tenants elsewhere are at their most precarious. DC-based geographer Amanda Huron refers to these processes as the production of an urban commons, which, although complex and contradictory, continues to constitute an alternative property relation forty years on.[38]

Social housing conversions are politically and architecturally interesting in part because they evince simultaneously radical and conservative elements. On the one hand, they are a radical reclamation of housing. Particularly in situations of landlord neglect and abandonment, tenants themselves have committed the labor to keep their buildings going, even in the absence of any compensation and often while continuing to pay rent to an absentee corporate body. By taking over their own housing, they are also reclaiming their own labor power and asserting a stake in the future of their home and their city. This is a concrete step toward deepening the meaning of a right to a home and enacting a right to the city.

But there can also be a conservative aspect to these conversions, both in terms of the built environment and the political stakes. Social housing conversions often involve interior renovations to make apartments more livable, but they rarely result in visible architectural changes to the built environment beyond better brick maintenance or perhaps green roofs. Whereas purpose-built social housing often proclaims its values through its architecture—whether that be bold brutalism, ostentatiously green design, or mock Tudor for the masses—these conversions are not about building the city as we collectively wish to see it so much as taking back the city as it has already been designed.

Deeper still, there can be a conservative underpinning to the "do it ourselves" ethos of social housing conversions. As historians Suleiman Osman[39] and Benjamin Holtzman[40] have argued, many of these conversions took place in the context of large-scale state retrenchment, when New York City was in fiscal crisis and the State of New York was imposing austerity. In popular programs of squatting, sweat equity, parks reclamation, and more, individuals and collectives built up a network of voluntary and cooperative programs to make up for the state's decline.

Some of these conversions had an anarchist dimension, particularly in the Lower East Side squats, where state power and private ownership were both rejected outright as offensive and outmoded. Other projects had a more liberal orientation toward "big government," seeing it as incompatible with community and likely to reproduce alienation in any large-scale planning. While neither approach is conservative in itself—and in fact some of it is quite radical—they both played into the public sector's retreat from housing production and helped cement the idea that nonstate means of stabilizing communities are inherently stronger than large-scale planning and public investment. Soon, bourgeois institutions like parks conservancies, business improvement districts, and grant-making foundations would build on some of the same arguments and circumstances and come to play an increasingly large role in urban governance.

Perhaps the best way to understand both the potential and the limitations of tenant-led social housing conversions is by comparison to workers who take over their employers' businesses. There is a long international history of firm mismanagement—or, in some cases, union demands that push companies beyond the limits of market logic—that has led bosses to exit business and workers to take over production. In my generation, perhaps the most iconic example is the Argentinian workers movement's factory takeovers in the wake of that country's 2001 financial crisis, as depicted in Avi Lewis and Naomi Klein's 2004 documentary, *The Take*. After assuming control of a business, workers must still maintain the shop and keep the plant running, but they can do so on terms that better conform to their own preferences. They cannot unilaterally exit the market system, which may result in some self-exploitation or even exploitation of others outside the cooperative structure, but they can assert their collective self-determination and make their own decisions.[41]

Similarly, tenants who take over their buildings must still think about costs, upkeep, labor, and self-governance. They cannot collectivize the world beyond their coop, but they can at least come to their own verdicts on how to maintain their buildings, where to put their savings, and how to deal with problems as they inevitably arise. The process is messy and contentious, without a doubt, but it is equally empowering. In Kim Stanley Robinson's climate fiction novel *New York 2140*, after two great floods, New Yorkers convert dozens of Midtown office towers into massive cooperative housing and rooftop-farming projects, and people move around the city on boats and rafts. But even in this imaginative and somewhat hopeful vision of the future, in which much of what we know about the world has been washed away, coop drama—like the mighty cockroach—remains everlasting.

For this model to work, we will need mass tenant organizing, buttressed by city and state governments willing to actually enforce the laws that constrain exploitation on the part of landlords—namely strong rent regulations and strict housing-quality code enforcement—and willing to pass policies like TOPA to transfer housing and budget for acquisitions, renovations, operating subsidies, and rental assistance. Celeste Hornbach, Oksana Mironova, Jacob Udell, and I call this combined approach building "pathways to social housing."[42] These roads will by no means be smooth, but they nonetheless show how we might move from the deplorable present into a cooperative future.

Conversions, however, make up a small portion of New York City's social housing stock. The vast majority of New York's social housing was built that way, and though some has been privatized, most of it remains social today.

Public housing is by far the biggest and most important social housing program New York has ever produced. With over 150,000 apartments in hundreds of developments across the five boroughs, the New York City Public Housing Authority's program is the largest in the country.[43] This is true not only in terms of the number of apartments—which may not be surprising, given that New York City is by far the largest municipality in the United States—but also by percentage of the total housing stock.[44] Ninety years ago, the city made a commitment to public provision of affordable housing, and while 13 percent of the stock has since been brought under private management through a local version of the federal Rental Assistance Demonstration program,[45] New York has refused to follow the mainstream American program of demolishing or privatizing most or all of its public housing.

Unlike most other cities, New York got its start with public housing before the federal government took on—and later abandoned—this role. The first public housing in New York City was municipal social housing. Originally planned as a conversion project, a stretch of Lower East Side tenements was purchased by the city from the Astor family. When renovation plans turned too costly, the city instead tore the buildings down and built new, similarly proportioned and aligned buildings known as "First Houses."

The model took off. The New Deal initiated a particular mode of public housing that emphasized "urban renewal" (or demolition of existing residential and industrial areas, often low income and home primarily to Black and immigrant households) and construction of low-income housing, with a one-to-one ratio of public demolition to public development. While left-oriented New York City mayors like Fiorello LaGuardia and Communist and Socialist Congress and city council members like Vito Marcantonio, Ben Davis, Pete Cacchione, and Baruch Vladeck (for whom a Lower East Side public housing development is named) might have wished for a better model, with public housing able to outbuild private housing and with a broader share of the city housed under its auspices, instead, the federalized system guided cities toward a tear-down and build-up model. This created a flood of internally displaced residents at a pace that constantly overwhelmed the city's resettlement authority.[46] But it also built up an enduring bulkhead of working-class communities spread across four-fifths of the city's community districts, and forming as much as a third of the rental-housing stock in neighborhoods like East Harlem.[47]

Since the program began, public housing has had its haters, and while it has valiantly persevered in New York, the model remains beleaguered. From the right, there are those who think the government has no business building, owning, or operating housing in the first place. From the left, there are those who say (fairly, in my opinion) that the program never went far enough, with design and budget guidelines that dictated cheap construction methods and led to segregation and substandard quality. Some public housing projects initially lacked such basics as toilet seats or closet doors. Coming from a mix of both perspectives, many espouse what urban critic Owen Hatherley has diagnosed as "the New York ideology," a semiconscious bias that sees big planning and big projects as inherently doomed, favoring instead the slow and iterative development its adherents depict as more organic.[48]

Indeed, chronic federal underfunding has led to a self-fulfilling prophecy, with deferred maintenance leading to dangerous and sometimes deadly conditions in some developments. Rather than understand this as the consequence of stingy and regressive budgeting, however, mainstream politicians and pundits have cast it as the inevitable outcome of public ownership.

But, like rent regulation, public housing is essential to New York City as we know it.

According to official statistics—which are universally understood to be an undercount—nearly 300,000 New Yorkers live somewhere in the public housing system.[49] If we are ashamed that New York City's homeless population is roughly the size of Boulder's entire population, we should be proud that the population living in New York City's public housing is roughly the size of Pittsburgh. Public housing provides a tremendous amount of stability to New York City's working class, and thus to the city as a whole.

Alongside public housing stand other models of purpose-built social housing in New York, some of which preceded even the development of First Houses. The first social housing developments in New York were limited-equity cooperative projects sponsored by working-class institutions in the central Bronx, the Lower East Side of Manhattan, and Sunset Park, Brooklyn. This model coalesced into the union cooperative movement, led by the garment workers and their United Housing Foundation (which built Bayard Rustin's home in Penn South) and joined by electrical workers, butchers, typesetters, furriers, and health care workers. All together, the model produced roughly 50,000 homes, designed to be affordable for working-class residents to buy, live in, and then pass on to other households in their same class position.

Many of these projects turned into cooperative villages, with not only shared open spaces and cultural facilities (like theaters, libraries, and meeting rooms) for residents to enjoy, but an entire solidarity economy ecosystem. Although none of these facilities existed all together in the same projects, New York City cooperative developments collectively maintained pharmacies, health clinics, day-care facilities and nursery schools, school buses, groceries linked to politically aligned farms upstate, furniture stores, bakeries, Kosher butchers, sports clubs, energy purchasing (and later power generation) schemes, newspapers, and—at least in one case—the development's own community alternative to the municipal police.[50] Writing about the electricians' cooperative development built over a golf course near Utopia Parkway in Queens, the labor journalist A. H. Raskin described its union sponsor as "the operator of an industry-financed welfare state that supplies cradle-to-grave protection for the families of 30,000 members."[51]

In addition to these union- and worker-centric cooperatives were projects developed by other limited-profit corporations, with similar affordability guidelines. Under the state's Mitchell-Lama program, union developers, nonprofits and other firms willing to limit their profits could develop limited-equity cooperatives and limited-cost rentals with public support in the form of tax breaks, bond financing, and low-interest loans. From the mid-1950s to the early 1980s, the program produced 69,000 cooperative apartments and 66,000 rental homes.

Looking back at her time growing up in a Mitchell-Lama cooperative, the author Jennifer Baum subtitled her book *Growing Up on the Upper West Side When Housing Was a Human Right*. This is a bit of knowing hyperbole—housing has never truly been treated as a human right in New York City—but this era of mass social housing production was perhaps the closest we have ever been, not only because social housing was plentiful, but because that very plentitude fostered a culture of care among those who enjoyed it.[52]

Crucially, however, the Mitchell-Lama program contained what policymakers call a "sunset" clause, allowing owners to exit the program after the mortgage is paid. Tenant activist John Leyva, however, urges us all to stop using this language to paint something so destructive and destabilizing as natural and inevitable. "I don't call it a sunset because sunsets are beautiful," he often says. "I call it a 'doomsday' clause."

Subsequent laws have made it harder to abandon affordability, but before those reforms were made, more than half of rentals and approximately 10 percent of coops left the program. Some have gone into rent stabilization, while others rent or sell for as much as the market allows.

Mitchell-Lama housing and union cooperatives remain extremely popular models in New York City, and this support stands as evidence that New Yorkers could embrace a return to large-scale social housing construction. Hundreds of thousands of New Yorkers have put themselves on waiting lists for social cooperative and public housing developments, each hoping their number is called so they can exit the anti–social housing landscape of profit-seeking landlords and grueling shelter stays. When cooperatives had lower barriers to exiting the program, the fact that few did suggests that most residents understand how the use value of home and community can outweigh the potential exchange value of windfall profits.[53] (The fact that so many Mitchell-Lama rental landlords opted out of the program demonstrates the opposite: that for landlords, their building's use value *is* its exchange value.) Every four years, mayoral candidates pledge to establish a "Mitchell-Lama 2.0," though none yet has followed through to deliver it.

As New Yorkers revisit past models of social housing construction, we also look abroad to cities and countries with far stronger track records of social sector development. In 2022, I was invited to join a delegation of New York City housing activists, including homeless and tenant leaders, organizers, politicians, and researchers, to spend a week studying Vienna's famously successful social housing model.

I was hesitant to attend; as a Jew, I was never comfortable celebrating twentieth-century Austria. I might have preferred a trip to Uruguay, where, since 1970, the Federation of Housing Cooperatives for Mutual Aid has presented one of the strongest—if less widely heralded—legacies of self-built cooperative social housing on the planet.

But I knew that the Vienna trip would become a touchstone of future housing politics in New York, and indeed, for its participants it has. We were exposed not just to well-designed, well-built, and well-maintained municipal social housing, some of it nearly 100 years old, but *so much* of it, seemingly everywhere throughout the city. Suddenly our 9 percent social housing stock seemed paltry compared to their 43 percent.[54]

The numbers only begin to capture the feeling of being in a city that treats housing as a human right—and, notably, a city with an even higher proportion of immigrants than our own.[55] In Vienna, homelessness is, indeed, rare and of short duration. Social housing is eligible to all after two years of stable residency, including in emergency shelters. The city is adding social housing all the time, and the old stock is not only maintained but improved, with rents falling over time as construction debts are repaid.

One day during the visit I set out on my own to look for a Jewish cemetery (which turned out to be fenced off because of repeated anti-Semitic graffiti attacks) and accidentally stumbled on a building that looked something like my own walk-up tenement in New York, only it was owned by the city and they had built an exterior glass elevator to make its upper floors accessible to elders and anyone who might struggle with multiple flights of stairs. Looking at that lift, I thought of my across-the-hall neighbor, Hassan, an elderly man who valiantly trudged up and down the stairs each day—increasingly with assistance from his family or me and my wife. Our building is far too narrow for an internal elevator, but it had never even occurred to me that, with the proper resources and regulations, we could put one outside and punch through the walls to create new entrances, saving Hassan (and eventually all of us) the struggle and danger of all those stairs.

Meanwhile, Vienna's new social housing developments—mostly limited-equity cooperatives built by highly regulated nonprofit entities, but also some built and owned by the city's housing authority—were decadently gorgeous. Chosen through a competitive process that values design as well as affordability, they often featured car-free streets, verdant balconies and roofs, energy-efficient building materials, solar power, communal kitchens and children's playrooms, and, in nearly every case, a sauna, a pool, or multiples of both. And perhaps most bafflingly, the Vienna model demands *less* subsidy on a per-resident basis than New York's housing. Why? Because, we were told by local planning officials, Vienna takes active measures to cool land and property values, then buys land and subsidizes construction for housing that is never meant to turn a profit—whereas we construct subsidy schemes meant to ensure profits for an array of stakeholders, from landowner to landlord.

On a trip to the museum inside Karl-Marx-Hof, the preeminent social housing development of the "Red Vienna" period (1918–1934), I remember stopping and staring intently at a photographic portrait of the project's self-defense brigade. They stood in a military formation with rifles in hand, aware enough of the fascist menace to start preparing but seemingly self-confident in their ability to ward it off. The past we know too well was their still-undetermined future. It was as humbling as it was horrifying to imagine what became of these young men just a few years later, and to contemplate our own existential ignorance of whatever future awaits us.

When our delegation returned home, it was clear to us that we had a long way to go to match what our comrades in Vienna had shown us. But it was also clear that for every aspect of the Vienna model, we had a diminished corollary. "New York as shitty Vienna," I began to call it in my head. We have public housing, but it has never been as well designed, built, or maintained. We have limited-equity coops built by limited-dividend companies, but we built far fewer of them, and we allowed some to go private. We have inclusionary zoning, but whereas their model requires two-thirds of the development to be social housing, ours only demands that one-third be targeted to tenants under a certain household income. We have rent control, but it covers less than half of the private rental stock. We spend city capital on housing, but we get less for our money because we refuse to decommodify most of the homes we invest in. We have a city-chartered nonprofit that can temporarily hold tax-foreclosed land and buildings, but we do not have a proper public land bank whose mission is to compile and acquire parcels before their value rises and put them toward social housing production.

Tenant and homeless groups got to work on envisioning a new social housing model for New York State, which could build on the successes of the past while improving on their shortcomings. The result is a bill that would create a Social Housing Development Authority for New York State, a democratically operated public entity designed in the spirit of the Labor Housing Conference. It could build new social housing as well as acquire buildings and oversee conversions. It would offer a way out of the interminable cycles of disinvestment and gentrification that have turned housing into a vehicle for upward and racialized wealth redistribution. It is not perfect, and as I write this it remains far from passing, but it is the first time in a generation (if not longer) that the New York housing left has collectively asserted a positive vision for new housing construction.

And we were not alone in doing so: around the country, city and state initiatives of various kinds have been experimenting with how to restart social housing production, from my birth state of Rhode Island, where Reclaim RI is fighting to transform the state's Department of Housing into a public developer with the power to build mixed-income public housing and preserve existing buildings, to Seattle, Washington, where residents voted to create and fund a new municipal social housing developer.[56] In all these cases of grassroots mobilization for social housing, organizers are rethinking the role of the state in housing and pushing back against a century of racist policy design and implementation.

The capitalist state is not going to simply embrace this transformation because it is the right thing to do. In fact, the state as we know it is constructed specifically to avoid this outcome. It could, however, be pushed into this position by an organized working class, who suffer under the status quo and are uniquely situated to both transform the state and to deliver on the full promise of democracy. As the British sociologist Ralph Miliband argued decades ago, although a "deep malaise, a pervasive sense of unfulfilled individual and collective possibilities penetrates and corrodes the climate of every advanced capitalist society," people still sought political transformation, in their homes and workplaces but also from the governments they live under. "It is towards the state," Miliband wrote, "that they are increasingly driven to direct their pressure; and it is from the state that they expect the fulfillment of their expectations."[57] If *this state* will not deliver a right to housing, we must do the work to bring about a state that will.

I am writing these words the day before the 2025 New York City primary election. Soon enough we will know the results of this contest, and of the general election to follow. But today, all that is still the future, and I can bask in the possibilities this blessed ignorance affords.

For the first time ever, tenant and homeless organizing has compelled *seven* mayoral candidates to pledge that they would freeze rent-stabilized rents, at least for the coming year. The leading left contender, Zohran Mamdani, pledged to freeze them for the entirety of his term. Two candidates—Mamdani and Brad Lander—put renewed and large-scale social housing conversion and construction at the heart of their plans. Most of the primary contenders support expanding municipal rental assistance. Today I cannot yet know whether one of these candidates or the man who promises none of these things—the once-disgraced ex-governor who holds a narrowing lead in the polls—will win.

The results tomorrow may be heartening or they may be dismaying. But from the standpoint of June 23, 2025, it is a tremendous success that the Tenant Bloc and other formations have successfully organized almost the entire field into committing to a progressive housing program. No one is running on an explicit and enforceable right to housing, but several are promising to expand the programs we would need to make that concept achievable.

On this day of electoral uncertainty, I allow myself to daydream about what life in a New York with a right to housing might be like. A New York City where everyone has a home they can afford. Where we can stay as long we wish and we can easily move whenever we choose. Where we can live together in intergenerational families of birth or of choice yet can still close a door and seek comfort in solitude. Where crises still strike but there are places to go for compassion and care, which will place us in permanent housing as quickly as possible. Where people can come together to deliberate and decide how we want our futures to unfold, without fear that taking such action might either raise our rent or lower our property values. Where communities can plan to combat climate change and protect ourselves against weather emergencies, including the possibility of moving to safer ground, with new social housing there to welcome us. Where the memories of mass homelessness, punishing rent burdens, poor conditions, segregation, and gentrification are all distant, and where anyone who ran for mayor on a platform of raising rents for tenants and lowering taxes for billionaires would be laughed off the debate stage.

This vision is distressingly distant from the city—let alone the world—we are living in today, where we chant our mantra that housing is a human right precisely because we live in a city, state, and country where it is manifestly not. These days, hitting "refresh" on any given news site risks plunging me deeper into anxiety bordering on panic, born not only from the fact that the world we inhabit is so far from the one we dream of, but that in many crucial ways that gap is widening with every passing moment. It is a deeply dispiriting time to be doing much of anything, let alone aspiring toward a right to housing.

And yet we continue on, reinventing the fight under whatever circumstances we find ourselves facing. This cyclicality conjures in me my mother's orientation toward the world—literally, toward the earth. She and her best friend have stewarded the same community garden plot for about thirty years. She is just as affected by the pain of the world as I am, but the force that keeps her going is the inherent optimism of the gardener, who, after every winter, labors to create life amid the ruins. Nothing renews her like the work of tending the land and watching seeds sprout miraculously each season, she and they and all of us lucky enough to live another day, never knowing what is to come.

This is the beauty of the present: I know something about the past; I know something about today; but I cannot say with any certainty that I know anything about the future. Perhaps it will be brighter. As historian Salar Mohandesi writes, "The emancipatory hypothesis cannot be proven one way or another—it comes down to a leap of faith."[58]

It is hard to hold hope that we are on the precipice of a great emancipatory turn, but I am increasingly finding that hope is beside the point. I take to heart the words of Mike Davis, an inveterate doomer but indefatigable partisan:

"Fight with hope, fight without hope, but fight absolutely."[59] The point is not to hope but to act regardless.

As I write those words, I realize that the term "to act" has a double valence. I meant to say "take action": don't just chant "Fight! Fight! Fight!" but *actually fight* for housing as a human right. But "acting" also means taking on a character and playing a part. This is sometimes how I feel these days: that my action is a kind of acting. Not that it is fake or performative, just that it involves some willful imagination. Acting the part of the activist who believes that we will win. Doing what needs to be done and delivering the lines that need to be spoken because that is what the moment calls for. Invoking a better world regardless of my imperfect faith that it will unfold. Acting is not a lie, but a discipline.

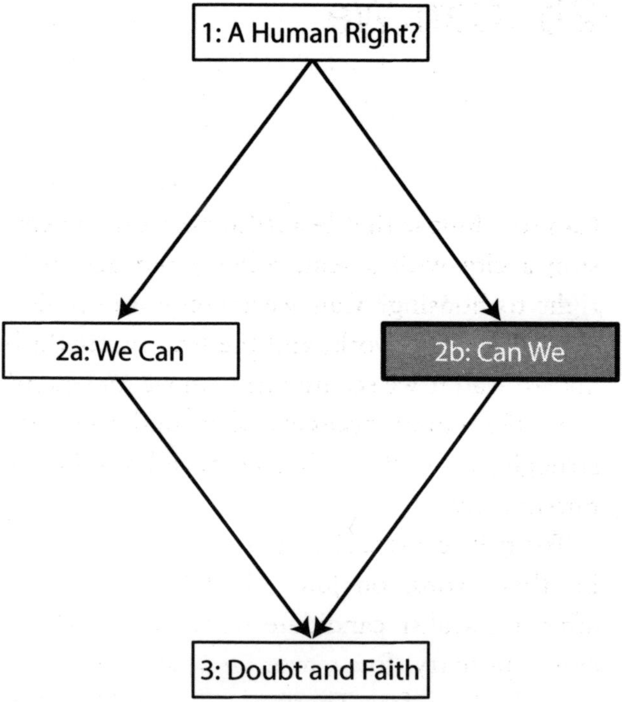
1: A Human Right?
2a: We Can
2b: Can We
3: Doubt and Faith

2b. Can We

Can we glimpse that beautiful horizon and envision a city with a real, robust, and actionable right to housing? Can we imagine the policies needed for it to work, and the lives we might be able to lead if we secured it? Can we understand both the moral necessity that underpins this struggle, as well as the headwind we face in pursuing it?

Today it seems easier than yesterday. I am writing these words on June 25, 2025, the morning after a socialist candidate clenched the Democratic primary for mayor and a horrid hack conceded his defeat. The victor, Zohran Mamdani, is not a neophyte embracing the mantle of the Democratic Socialists of America (DSA), but rather an active DSA member whose entire political career has been intertwined with the New York

City branch's post-2016 rebirth and growth. The headline in Liza Featherstone's *Jacobin* column this morning reads, "At a Bleak Political Moment, Zohran Mamdani Offers Hope."[1] In many ways, this is the greatest degree of political optimism I have experienced in years.

But I cannot believe with perfect faith that a real right to housing is anything the state, market, and social institutions we know could plausibly produce and protect, nor can I predict that any sufficient transformation of those institutions is brewing. Better leadership and governance will help tremendously to prevent conditions from worsening and will be essential for any further push in the right direction. I refuse to suppress my own enthusiasm for this socialist victory. And yet I also refuse to burden this triumph with the weight of impossible expectations.

My primary reluctance comes from the power of the real estate state: a confluence of state power and real estate capital that pursues a political and planning agenda of surging land and property values.[2] The real estate state has become particularly central to local urban governance in part because of the collapse or dispersion of previous alignments of capital and state power, none of which were particularly pleasant or progressive but which offered a substantial counterweight to the property lobby, which popular movements could at times leverage to their advantage.

In the absence of this competition, particularly in places that experienced profound deindustrialization during the second half of the twentieth century (when New York City lost over 700,000 manufacturing jobs[3]), cities experienced three types of vacuums. There was a spatial vacuum: What would take the place of former manufacturing and distribution sites? In many cases, the answer was high-end real estate. There was an economic vacuum: What would fill the employment and revenue base previously backed by the industrial sector? The jobs would primarily come from the low-wage service sector, while the revenue would increasingly come from property taxes. There was a political vacuum: In the absence of industry and industrial unions, who would set the planning agenda? In many cases, the answer was real estate, supported at times by segments of the social sector (namely the unions whose members build and work in high-end projects and the nonprofits who form revenue-sharing partnerships with developers).

Taken together, this represented a structural shift in power toward the urban real estate sector, and along with it a significant shift in growth-seeking investment capital toward not only real estate in general, but urban housing in particular. As Aaron Benanav and others have shown, when overall rates of profit fall—as, we are told, they have a tendency to do over time[4]—nervous investors shift their capital away from the sectors they had previously supported and toward increasingly speculative (and thus increasingly collapse-prone) asset sectors, including for-profit real estate.[5]

None of this is immutable, and in fact social movements and progressive politicians in cities like New York have put in place programs that successfully contest real estate's total hegemony. New York City's public housing was not demolished and privatized in mass the way it was around the country, and rent stabilization covers a tremendous portion of the housing stock. But the city remains highly dependent on real estate tax revenue to fund nearly everything we do.

Revenue from New York City's property taxes forms a plurality of the city's income and covers nearly 30 percent of the city's operating budget; thus, like virtually all US municipalities, New York City is structurally dependent on the growth and stability of its property tax base.[6] Nearly the same proportion of the city's operating budget comes as categorical grants from the federal and state governments, with much of the state money itself derived from federal sources, putting a rebel city at risk if higher orders of government oppose its agenda.[7] (Lest we forget, the current president is a former New York City real estate developer and racist landlord.)

The city needs all this money not just to maintain a police force the size of a small army but also to fund essential social programs that the left values equally to housing, such as public health, public schools, public parks, public libraries, public welfare, and more. In 2025, the New York City Department of Education budget was more than four times the size of the Police Department's budget.[8] For all this to hold up, cities need the assessed value of real estate to grow without pause. Otherwise, they will have to repeatedly raise property taxes on buildings with stagnant exchange values, find another funding source, or cut back on essential public goods.

Under this logic, any program that substantially challenges the price and primacy of urban real estate—as a program of more stringent rent controls, more intensive housing code enforcement, more extensive social housing conversions, and more expansive social housing construction would definitionally do—threatens to undermine the fiscal base of the local state in question. We could construct a more progressive system of property taxes, with the wealthy paying a higher share and working people paying less, but still, the high end of the market would have to keep delivering for the system to keep standing. Going in the other direction and decommodifying housing altogether would reduce property tax revenue to near null. Cities could find other ways to raise revenues, but under the current urban system, nothing works—from the public services we love to the carceral systems we hate—without stable or rising property values.

Not only are municipal budgets backed by private real estate growth, but so are many families' finances. This is the case across the country more than in majority-renter New York City, but even here one-third of residents (over one million households) are homeowners. For most, their property is not just their most valuable asset, it is the bedrock foundation for their children's education and for their own future retirement. They take a second mortgage on their home to pay for their children's college (as my parents did), and they must sell their homes for a substantial profit in order to afford senior housing and healthcare, or to leave something to their economically precarious children.

Lisa Adkins, Melinda Cooper, and Martijn Konings refer to this as a component of "the asset economy," in which "sustained inflation of property values over several decades has fundamentally shifted the social class structure, from a logic that was structured around employment towards one that is organized around participation in asset ownership and appreciation."[9] As Cooper further develops in her subsequent book, *Counterrevolution,* this asset economy was undergirded by wholesale cuts to public programs intended to boost wages and welfare, alongside rising spending (or tax noncollection) intended to boost asset prices in housing and stocks.[10]

American social security has never been totally sufficient to its task, leaving union-bargained pensions to fill the gaps. But unionization rates have plummeted and, despite recent pro-union enthusiasm, have not bounced back to anything close to the levels seen in the mid-twentieth century. Today, just one in ten American workers belongs to a union, leaving relatively few to benefit from the security of a defined-benefit pension.[11]

Union pensions, meanwhile, are essentially required to behave like corporate investment vehicles. Since 1974, when the Employee Retirement Income Security Act went into effect (in part to prevent unions from colluding with organized crime on speculative development projects like Las Vegas casinos, as depicted in Martin Scorsese's films *Casino* and *The Irishman*), unions must maintain a distance from their pension fund investments, which are expected to produce reliably high rates of returns. This in turn drives "labor's capital"[12] toward investing in economically competitive but hyper-exploitive nonunion firms, as well as in socially harmful corporate real estate schemes.

According to sociologist Michael McCarthy, "fund investments were directed into real estate, where prices were skyrocketing. Eventually, leading up to the financial crisis of 2008, they were drawn toward increasingly speculative purchases of junk bonds and exotic financial instruments such as subprime mortgages."[13] The California public sector pension fund, for example, invested in massive real estate firms whose business model included displacing retirees from low-cost homes—in other words, paying for pensions by evicting pensioners.[14] The very means to make up for our country's paltry social security system, then, is inflating our real estate sector and driving home prices even higher. Property owners and union members alike (sometimes one and the same, but in New York often not) are thus incentivized to equate rising property values with security in old age.

City planners are thus tasked with making housing more affordable to residents at the same time as it makes housing more valuable to owners, a contradiction that cannot easily be squared. Making housing affordable—let alone transforming the system such that housing is an actionable right—would necessarily also make it less profitable. This means devaluating one of the global economy's primary asset classes, cities' principal budgeting backstop, unions' financial bedrock, and families' private safety nets.

It is not just property in the abstract that is a problem but also property in the particular. The geographic specificity of housing makes its guarantee a colossally complex prospect.

This facet of housing politics was made clear to me by my late mentor, Tom Waters, who pointed out that unlike some other types of welfare provision, housing has to go somewhere and stay there, and the people who dwell in it shape their lives around it. It may determine their social networks, their schools, their political representation, their access to transit, their leisure activities, even their literal view of the city. As a physical assemblage of land, labor, and materials, to which people hold a lifetime of topophilic ties and emotional associations, housing has a stronger geographical dimension than other aspects of urban life and welfare policy.[15]

Hospitals need to be sited someplace too, but hospital users hope not to spend a great deal of time there—they simply need them to be there when and where they need them. Food must be sold or distributed somewhere, but people care mostly about that location in relation to their home. Like housing, food and healthcare are human rights in the sense that without them we will die, and the rights to food and healthcare are enmeshed in the same international legal declarations of the right to housing. They should be far simpler to guarantee because they do not have the same spatial specificity as housing—and yet, in this country, they are not. This makes the dream of a right to housing, with all its militant particularisms,[16] seem even more remote.

In the context of an asset economy, and one in which homes (or, in their commodity form, real estate) are the central asset, the geographic nature of housing is expressed via an endless parade of site-specific skirmishes: fights over what gets built where, over what is torn down and what is preserved, over the politics of place through the medium of price. These battles are perhaps most pitched over the siting of homeless shelters, which, despite our city's long-established right to shelter, can still inspire riotous behavior from unexpected quarters. In 2024, a Democratic city council member protesting a proposed shelter in her district literally bit and drew blood from a police officer—an action that might have gotten a Black Lives Matter protester sentenced to years in prison but came with no consequences in this case.

This kind of mania commonly accompanies the provision of a type of shelter already guaranteed by judicial order in New York City. Imagine the proliferation of site fights that would erupt if the city took seriously its responsibility to permanently house not only the historically high 100,000 people sleeping each night in our homeless shelters, but also the additional 200,000 functionally homeless and living in overcrowded and precarious quarters,[17] the more than 180,000 households waiting on the public housing waiting list,[18] and the over 600,000 who recently applied for rental assistance when the Section 8 voucher waiting list reopened for applications.[19] (Granted, there is some overlap between these groups.) The city, already tightly built out over most of its land mass, still needs to build or otherwise produce a plethora of homes to house the people who desperately need them, let alone to improve the housing of millions more who deserve much better than what they have today.

Of course, New York City *has* built mass social housing at various points in the twentieth century, including far more public housing, subsidized rentals, and limited-equity cooperatives than any other city in the country. But although this housing rightly remains among the New York left's proudest achievements, much of it was built through "urban renewal" actions that the left also abhors.[20] Although some social housing projects took creative advantage of vacant or underused locations, like a golf course in the case of the electrical workers' Electchester in Queens or a failed amusement park in the case of the garment workers' Coop City in the Bronx, many others were built by tearing down buildings (sometimes substandard, sometimes perfectly fine) that housed other working-class tenants, few of whom were then able to return to the improved housing built over their former homes.

In New York City, just 15 percent of those displaced by "urban renewal" were allowed to move into the buildings that went up on the site of their former homes. Another 35 percent moved into public housing elsewhere, sometimes quite far from their former homes and social bonds, and often on the site of other poor tenants' prior removal. The remaining 50 percent ended up in yet another substandard private building, deepening the city's geography of racial segregation.[21] When it was union-based developers who initiated this kind of displacement for their own social housing projects, historian Roberta Gold argues that they "built self-identified 'communities of working people' for their own members at the expense of working people further down the ladder. They pitted tenant against tenant, worker against worker, and it was the relatively secure tenants and workers who won out."[22]

When I was writing my doctoral dissertation on New York City unions' and nonprofits' complex and contradictory political orientations toward the real estate industry, I came across a box of documents collected by the Met Council on Housing, New York's longest-standing citywide tenants union, kept in New York University's Tamiment Archive of the US radical left. The box contained flyers and newspaper clippings documenting the site fight around Penn South, a large complex of limited-equity cooperative apartments in Manhattan's Chelsea neighborhood. Penn South is often viewed with pride as one of the biggest and best social housing developments in the city, a monument to the mid-century garment workers union's commitment to building affordable cooperatives for workers around the city in a neighborhood that is now among the most expensive in the city.

Combing through the files, I found that not only were roughly 7,000 working-class tenants displaced to build housing for 7,000 almost entirely different working-class tenants, but that some of those displaced for Penn South had already been displaced by previous urban renewal actions, including some sponsored by the same unions responsible for this project. One site tenant told of being relocated to the Penn South area after being evicted by the garment workers' Seward Park project the prior year:

> I was forced out of that site when I was served with a dispossess before being offered another apartment. When I told the relocation authorities that they were sending me into another area where the buildings were going to be demolished, they told me it was the best they could do for me.[23]

I knew that I might find anguished stories of displaced tenants. I did not expect to see the issue framed in some of the exact same terms as development fights that were happening in New York City in 2018. In both, the same questions were asked: For whom is this project affordable? How do the proposed costs compare to the rents tenants are currently paying? Who will be forced to move in order to make room for growth? Who has a legitimate claim to the land? How can we make room for the housing we need without victimizing those living in the worst housing today? It was exactly the same framing, separated by six decades and several political regimes. While there could be something comforting about knowing that today's struggles are ones we have had to grapple with in the past, there is also something deeply dismaying about realizing that we are still fighting the same fights as always, and that many of the greatest achievements of our movements were subject to the same contradictions and inequities we rail against today.

Certain things just do not change: the city was crowded then, and it is crowded today. Large-scale development engenders myriad site fights, including among working-class people and institutions as well as in more direct class conflicts between the rich and the poor.

One thing that has changed, in New York City and many other places, is that since the 1970s, we have been far more willing to subsidize housing if it results in profits for some powerful bloc. There was profit involved in earlier rounds of social housing productions—investors bought bonds to finance public housing construction, and banks collected interest on cooperatives' mortgages—but the scale of accumulation has grown tremendously. Labor activist and theorist Kim Moody aptly titled his book on this transition *From Welfare State to Real Estate*.[24]

For many years, New York City has gleefully foregone more money on property tax breaks for largely high-end private development than any branch of government spent on New York's public and subsidized housing.[25] (It is worth noting that one of the early boosters of this approach was a young Donald Trump, who sought and largely received every tax break on the books in order to develop his Manhattan luxury real estate portfolio.[26]) The federal government spends far more on programs to subsidize private landlords than it spends on public housing owned and operated by government-chartered authorities. Most of the affordable housing that has been built for the past forty years across the United States has been financed by the Reagan-era Low-Income Housing Tax Credit, a Rube Goldberg machine that subsidizes housing by selling investors the right to reduce their taxes.

This approach is often pitched as more fiscally responsible, in the "business-knows-best" vein, but it does not necessarily save money. The city of Vienna, world famous for its vast and high-quality social housing, spends a lot on this system, but it still pays less per resident than New York City. The difference is that we are subsidizing land and housing for profit, which turns out to be tremendously expensive, especially over time.

This is a structural problem of the capitalist state: its leaders and planners must ensure healthy profits for real estate in order to sustain a fiscal base and maintain elite support, while also addressing affordability in order to maintain popular legitimacy. As a result of this bind, most of our means for incentivizing housing affordability also bid up land prices, paradoxically ensuring that making housing cheap also means making it more expensive. This leads straight into the kinds of cost spirals that both city planners and individual renters or home buyers have become accustomed to. If the fiscal cost is exorbitant, though, the political cost of subsidizing profits is far lower for all scales of American government than creating a system that would truly confront, compete with, and rein in some of the world's most powerful industries.

Real estate and finance capital have constructed a sort of ransom scheme: deal with the housing problem through means that benefit us or face the risk of a capital strike. A coordinated capital strike, in which investors refuse to buy municipal bonds, developers refuse to build, lenders refuse to lend, landlords refuse to maintain their buildings, and governments and unions are pressured to relent on policies and contracts that organized capital determines are too costly, is not an everyday occurrence, but it is a historical fact, and, when successful, it can lead to a full-on fiscal and legitimacy crisis of the state.[27] To some degree the New York City fiscal crisis that helped usher in the neoliberal era was, among other things, a form of capital strike against the city's labor and welfare regimes.[28]

Tenants, too, can manufacture crises that we hope will result in serious and long-term shifts in the way the state relates to housing as a source of profit versus housing as a human right. One such strategy would be for renters to organize at the building, legislative, and electoral levels for maximal tenant protections and housing code enforcement, constraining landlords' ability to discipline tenants through rent hikes and retaliatory evictions while ensuring that landlords live up to the letter of the law in terms of housing quality maintenance. When landlords fail to do so, the state would be in a position to seize the building through eminent domain or a similar process, or to finance its purchase on the part of the tenants themselves or a social housing entity of the residents' choosing.[29]

For this to work, however, the state must be willing to take a sustained pummeling from tens of thousands of landlords who would see their profits squeezed and their investments seized. The easier course would be to either back off on the tenant protections and code enforcement or to grant even greater subsidies to landlords struggling to hold on to their buildings in the face of this regulatory squeeze.

Given the result of the recent New York City Democratic mayoral primary, this may not be a theoretical question at all. A leftist mayor of New York City might argue that pursuing this aggressive push toward social housing conversions would help the city's tenants—who make up two-thirds of the city's population—actualize their right to the city. This language harkens back to the French near-revolution of 1968 and the push to seize control over the city away from capitalist and political elites and instead to radically democratize what we now dryly call "planning" and might otherwise simply think of as "the future."

Landlords, surely, would protest that such a program might violate *their* right to the city. Violating landlords' rights, however, is more of a feature than a bug of a real program for a right to the city. Part of the premise is that as long as landlords maintain such a structural stranglehold over renters and cities, urban dwellers' democratic rights and capacities will remain severely constrained.

But the landlords' hue and cry point to a practical problem for anyone planning to institute a right to the city program: What if we profoundly disagree on what kind of city we want to see? If every individual, or even every community, has this right, what do we do about irreconcilably different desires and visions for the city? What happens when divergent fractions of "the people" want to demolish and preserve the same structure? What about communities with radically different values but strong claims to the same place? Such a scenario is not only common, it is replicated on every block of this beautifully complicated city.

A few years ago I reviewed the excellent book *A Fortress in Brooklyn* for the magazine *Jewish Currents*.[30] The book tells the story of the establishment and development of the Satmar Hasidic enclave in southern Williamsburg, Brooklyn, and the conflicts and coalitions such a project engendered—conflicts and coalitions between members of the Satmar community, between Satmar Hasidim and other Orthodox groups, between Satmar Hasidim and neighboring non-Jewish communities, and between Satmar Hasidim and various scales of government. It seemed to me that the book was the story of this particular community's long-term fight for their right to the city. But the version of city life Satmar Hasidim sought is not entirely compatible with the city desired by others—or even by all the members of their own group—and so it engendered a fight, sometimes pitched admirably and sometimes ignobly.

It is easy to see Satmar Hasidim as exceptional, given their insularity and distinctive religious practices, but the book hammered home the sense that in a city as complex as New York, such conflicts are inevitable, and democracy does not give us clear ways to sort through them. Surely we can make our systems more responsive, but the bigger and more radically diverse a place is—two things we, on the left, should not only want but demand from our cities!—the harder it is to imagine everyone equally sharing this right to the city.

A while back I was on a panel with the great urban theorist Peter Marcuse, following a screening of the documentary *My Brooklyn* at a City University of New York campus, and a student asked how community control would work in a city like ours with such extreme inequalities. Wouldn't the rich get to control their own neighborhoods in a way that excludes the rest of us? Marcuse asked the questioner to imagine instead if we treated community control along the same lines as taxation and applied the modifier "progressive" to both.

In progressive taxation, those who make the most pay the most; in progressive community control, those communities who have had the greatest say for the longest time should have less say in the planning system, and those who have been denied this opportunity for collective self-determination should have more.

This is a valiant principle, and it was a brilliant answer to the question, but it becomes difficult to map this proposal onto real communities. While income is a quantitative metric, history is not. Though both extremes surely exist in most cities, there is a vast and complicated space between places that have enjoyed historically high levels of political privilege and those that have been demonstrably fucked over time and again. It would be extremely difficult to come to a consensus about the relative degree of privilege that all the in-between places hold.

None of this is to say that we cannot dream of a better world, including a New York City with a true right to housing. Our left movements today are brimming with hearty visions that reimagine the world as we know it and offer up a radically redesigned future.

We have degrowth communists who picture a postcapitalist future in which the ecologically unsound imperative to grow is replaced by a commitment to living with more or less what we have and can sustainably reproduce, and a corresponding shift in values away from the drive to accumulate and toward the drive to appreciate. On the other side of the environmentalist left ledger, we have eco-modernists promising scientific and technological solutions to climate change and other environmental catastrophes, putting their faith in a form of humanism that believes in our power to overthrow the capitalist death drive and channel our collective capital, time, and energy into projects that promise full employment and full housing on a planet that is full of life.

We have anarcho-communists and communization adherents who eschew the normative modes of politics (electoralism, policy campaigns, party politics, certain forms of trade unionism, and so on) and emphasize semi-spontaneous collective revolts in times of acute crisis and who build, in the meantime, communes and mutual aid networks that operate parallel to the sclerotic society they regard as doomed. We have techno-optimistic leftists embracing the somewhat impish slogan of "fully automated luxury communism" and envisioning a science fiction–inspired post-scarcity utopia wherein, thanks largely to not-yet-invented technologies and a reordering of society around these newfound capacities, everyone has not only what they need but what they desire, the planet is spared from the ravages of greenhouse gases and other capital-inflicted poisons, and all of humanity is liberated from the shackles of wage labor and from all undesirable forms of work.

We have resurgent anarcho-syndicalists and council communists attempting to forge anti-capitalist corners outside the mainstream labor movement that aim to inspire workers to abandon all fealty to their employers, to the unions that enter into inherently limiting contracts with them, and to the capitalist state itself and building instead a new society from the shop floor (and farm, and community center, and so on) up. We have believers in a repaved parliamentary path to socialism, which views the Democratic Party as a potentially potent but hollow husk to be repopulated by democratic socialist movement candidates who can enter the halls of power with the backing of a mass base and retool public capacities toward liberatory ends.

On the housing front, we have dreams of popular uprisings occupying the largely empty luxury towers that loom over the New York City skyline on dystopian drags like Midtown Manhattan's "Billionaires' Row" and squatting the warehoused tenement apartments that are scattered about certain gentrified neighborhoods, converting them all into a people's paradise. From a more developmentalist strain, we get a redirection of the contemporary housing culture war, away from the accusatory slur of Not in My Backyard (NIMBY) and the proudly worn moniker of Yes in My Backyard (YIMBY), and toward an alternative horizon: Public Housing in My Backyard (PHIMBY) or Social Housing in My Backyard (SHIMBY), imagining a socialist state willing to break with the real estate state and build all the housing we need in the public domain. And from both camps, we hear a familiar battle cry: Fight! Fight! Fight! Housing is a human right!

These are but simplified capsule summaries of complex concepts forming a necessarily incomplete survey of the landscape. The point I wish to convey is that sundry streams of radicalism abound, all with long legacies on the historical left (often stretching back before the linguistic shortcuts of "left" and "right" took hold). For all this multiplicity, however, there is a profound sense of despair at their prospects, for the foreseeable future at least. These are all visions of what *could* arise, but the clock of the world keeps ticking, and it seems to be pointing us, grimly, in the opposite direction.

The electoral left, best characterized by the remarkably successful New York City branch of the DSA, can probably point to the most visible victories—and, in fact, this is a paramount part of their success. Elections are won or lost, and they always come with some degree of public participation and media scrutiny. DSA leadership knows this and understands that elections are not just a means toward policy ends, and ways to reconstitute the personnel and ideological spectrum of our representative democracy, but also ways to build a membership around a project with visible stakes and clear outcomes. But winning elections—even major ones, like the 2025 New

York City mayoral contest—is not the same as achieving a transformation.

We can and should point to important policy achievements enabled by having socialists in office, and we should work toward many more, including by electing more socialists into office. But the electoral endgame has always seemed elusive to me. One hundred years ago, the left debated whether or not it was possible to have socialism in one country. Today, we seem to be debating whether or not it is possible to have socialism in one city—only we are mostly *not* having that debate, and instead we're trying to find out anyway for lack of any other option.

It strikes me that even in the realm of fiction, I cannot think of many recent creative imaginings of how we might bring about a large-scale left futurity without relying on a parade of intermediate horrors. Over the past decade, I have encountered two great novels that demonstrated this tendency in reimagining New York City several decades from today.

The first was Kim Stanley Robinson's *New York 2140*,[31] published in 2017, which imagines a city transformed by extraordinary floods.

Manhattan's streets are largely now canals. The office buildings have become residential coops, with farms and renewable energy on the roofs and communal kitchens below. Inequality remains, with the wealthy guarding their high-rises on Manhattan's highest ground, the northern reaches of Washington Heights and Inwood, and the poor scrounging on makeshift boats. The finance industry persists as well, perhaps the clearest sign that we have not entered into a communist utopia, and it seeks ways to profit from the cooperators' new mode of being. But there is a radically communitarian element to New York City life, an acceptance that everything must change in order for all of us to survive, and an inspiring crop of rising social movements and political figures aiming to reshape the economy from the local to the global.

There is a lot to be inspired by in this novel, and perhaps its refusal to go full-on utopian makes it easier to enter into its world free from toxic skepticism or needling what-aboutism. In New York City, in the distant but still fathomable year of 2140, social reproduction seems to have been largely communalized, at least for much of the middle class. The formerly unpaid, individualized, and gendered work of cooking and childcare is now the responsibility of the cooperative as a whole. An ecological consciousness pervades everyday urban life. But all this comes about only *after* not just one but two horrific floods wash away much of the city, destroying lives, burying histories underwater, and summoning a massive calamity that forces a reordering of society and state.

The second novel presents a timeline that is more quickly approaching and portrays both an even worse set of coming catastrophes and an even bolder array of post-crisis possibilities. M. E. O'Brien and Eman Abdelhadi's *Everything for Everyone: An Oral History of the New York Commune, 2052–2072*[32] is an ingeniously structured novel that places the narrators fifty years into the future from the book's publication in 2022, soliciting oral histories of how that future came about from a wide array of participants.

The story they tell begins from a premise that communization theory is essentially correct. The new world does not come about through elections, parties, manifestos, or policies; it comes about by the people themselves forming collectives, fighting fascists, establishing home bases, liberating the caged, and ultimately communizing all aspects of life, from food and childcare to housing and socially necessary labor. The way we live today, with compulsory wage labor and undervalued unwaged labor, with insular biological families responsible for rearing and raising children, with landlords charging rent to access the means of human survival and homemaking, is seen as patently absurd, even unthinkable to those too young to have ever experienced it. This is a world transformed, with only pockets of rightist resistance holding onto embattled bases of power.

But before any of this occurs, the entire world suffers a litany of horrors. I will not spoil the plot, which emerges in nonlinear fragments told by various characters throughout the course of the interviews, but a few of the terrors that take place between the reader's already fairly dystopian present and the authors' utopian future include nuclear war, genocide, religious tyranny, slavery, floods, fires, famine, and economic collapse. All these things are disturbingly present in the world we know today, but in order for communes to be established in nearly every corner of the world, the horror is first intensified and generalized, made inescapable, qualitatively and quantifiably worsened. The authors are not accelerationists, gleefully welcoming these terrors as the only way to bring about societal transformation, but, rather, they present it as what we all might soon be facing—if we are fortunate enough not to be living it already.

Two months after *Everything for Everyone* was published, the great socialist critic and scholar-activist Mike Davis died. He had warned the world that his end was near, and so in the year before his passing a great many authors and activists paid Davis tribute. One offering, written by *Jacobin* editor Micah Uetricht, noted that over the course of Davis's published works, including over twenty books—most of them still widely read and revered, by me and a great many others—Davis transitioned from framing organized workers and the working class in general as the necessary historical protagonist of social, economic, and political transformation to instead presenting nature itself as the greatest force of social destruction and rebirth. As Uetricht wrote, "Davis started his career writing about workers' failed attempts to change the world; now he was insisting on the raw, terrifying power of ecology to shape and reshape the world as it pleases, with little concern for whatever petty exertions humans were engaged in."[33] This did not engender a shift in Davis's politics or desires for the US and every other country, but rather a shift in his understanding of what might be most likely to bring about change. His was not a call for the workers of the world to disunite, but rather for us all to understand why a workers' revolution was not forthcoming, in this country at least, and to understand that a wholly different and altogether alarming type of transformation seemed to be happening throughout the world.

These works call to mind an oft-quoted adage, usually attributed to Fredric Jameson and linked to works of popular philosophy by Slavoj Žižek and Mark Fisher: that "it's easier to imagine the end of the world than the end of capitalism."[34] That pithy and tragic phrase continues to resonate widely because it is so clearly true, and therefore so deeply distressing. It seems to me that the novels discussed above offer a new synthesis of this sentiment, even as they aim to push past it: the easiest way to imagine the end of capitalism is via the end of the world.

The systems and institutions we have, those we are imbricated with and implicated in, are more plausibly leading us toward apocalypse than utopia, and it is hard to know what to do about it besides brace for impact and prepare to build a better world to come.

Part of this palpable panic is that we are running out of time. If large-scale leftist transformation (be it parliamentary or insurrectionary) seems unlikely in the short term, conjuring the long-term offers few comforts. In 1923, John Maynard Keynes famously quipped that "the *long run* is a misleading guide to current affairs. *In the long run* we are all dead."[35] True as this is, the long run feels shorter today than it did one hundred years ago. Humanity—or some large fraction of it—might not survive climate change in time for much of a long term to be plausible.

In her illuminating book *Doppelganger*, Naomi Klein at one point describes a feeling of political despair so prevailing that it destabilizes her entire worldview. Best known as the author of books on corporate malfeasance and popular resistance, particularly focused on the perpetrators of climate change and the left's efforts to counter them, Klein admits that she was beginning to feel as if the ground below her was disappearing. The proximate cause was the apparent defeat of mass projects like Bernie Sanders's presidential runs, Black Lives Matter, and the movement to enact a Green New Deal. In the wake of those lows, however, her deeper woe concerned the way participants in those movements turned on one another, often in public, and often online. It was all a mess, and in the meantime, the countdown to climate catastrophe was barreling ahead. Disaster seemed imminent, and no solution seemed plausible.

"For me," Klein writes, "it meant that I had run out of halfway-credible pathways away from disaster to offer. I no longer saw how we could avoid the social and ecological outcomes that so many of us most fear." Not only her career but her identity and ontology were built around the idea that while very bad things were happening and worse were in the works, popular movements could step into the breach and turn the course of history in the opposite direction. But recent events challenged that faith. "That was the deepest source of my vertigo," she continues. "Who was I without that story of plausible salvation to share?"[36]

Reading this passage, toward the end of an already frightening book, I felt a strange comfort. If even Naomi Klein felt this way, it made sense that I was feeling it too. It was a validation, coming from a writer and activist who had previously emphasized collective possibility over certain peril—an emphasis I had always appreciated but could no longer so confidently share.

This is why, no matter how much I regard them as profound works of political art, I could not draw hope from *New York 2140* and *Everything for Everyone*. To coin a tautology: as things are getting worse on this planet, things are getting worse on this planet. Temperatures and tides are rising, and so too are fascist parties, border walls, arms shipments, eugenic pseudosciences, retrograde gender dogmas, entrenched oligopolies, and parasitic technologies. Somebody blew up the crisis-to-solidarity pipeline, and now it feels far from certain that up from the wreckage will emerge a red rose.

Certainty, we should already understand, was never the point. If history and geography were formulaic and predictable, there would be little point in politics. Stuart Hall urged the left to embrace a "Marxism without guarantees" over any functionalist formulations of the future.[37] As if to drive that lesson literally home to me, just before I moved to my current apartment, geographer Christian Anderson published an entire book about my specific street under the title *Urbanism without Guarantees*, which argued that gentrification is not a unidirectional and inevitable force.[38]

But there is certainty, which should always be contested in the political realm, and there is confidence, which should generally be cultivated in our movements. I think many of us are losing not only the confidence that we will win much of what we are fighting for today, but also any assurance that if we win some of our campaigns—particularly those over public policy—our institutions can support them into the future.

In political discussions, be they theoretical or practical, we often find ourselves invoking the abstraction of "the state," by which we generally mean the bodies and institutions of government and authority. (Once, during a class, Stanley Aronowitz said to me, without much further explanation, that "Columbia University is the state, too," so I don't mean to define "the state" here too narrowly. Still, when we talk about the state, we're mostly talking about the layers of governments with authority over a particular territory, or about governments in the abstract.)

I do this all the time. I can very well say right now that the state should and could codify a right to housing and take radical action to achieve it, including covering the cost of housing for those who can't afford it, limiting landlords' control over rent hikes, converting anti–social housing into social housing, and building beautiful, green social housing developments for all to thrive in and enjoy. But in making statements like these, I muddle the distinction between *the state* in theory and *this state* that we live under. *The state* could do all these things, and some states do (though vanishingly few do all of them well). *This state* does some of them, fairly poorly and incompletely, and is likely incapable of doing them all while retaining its fiscal basis and political legitimacy.

This is not to say that we are not or should not be trying. In fact, that is what I spend most of my time doing, day in and day out.

As I write these words today in New York City, we have in Zohran Mamdani a Democratic mayoral nominee who has committed to freezing the rent for the city's nearly one million rent-stabilized apartments, not just for one year but for each year of his mayoralty—something I am reasonably sure no one in his position has ever promised before. We have bills introduced in the city council, the state legislature, and even in the US Congress that would pave the pathways to social housing. The Tenant Opportunity to Purchase Act would give tenants across New York State the chance and resources to either buy their buildings and convert them into permanently affordable cooperatives or to select a purchaser of their choosing to run it as a not-for-profit or public rental. The Social Housing Development Authority bill would create a new public developer for New York State, which—with the democratic participation of tenants and workers, as well as planners and political appointees—would be empowered to both acquire existing buildings and convert them into social housing and to design and build new social housing complexes from the ground up. In Congress, we have the HOME Act, a bill that would create a social housing authority for the entire country, which could finance locally planned building and conversion projects across urban, suburban, rural, and Indigenous territories. We have any number of bills tagged as part of a Green New Deal, including Green New Deal for Public Housing legislation that would invest in environmentally friendly retrofits for existing social housing developments.

There is no legal or technical reason the state (the City of New York, the State of New York, or the US federal government) could not pass these bills. In one form or another, I truly believe they will! (The city and state ones, anyway—Congress is likely a lost cause for a while.) But do I expect the City and State of New York, even if led by better politicians, to go all the way to full decommodification and euthanize the for-profit real estate industry, which supplies the plurality of local tax revenues, is responsible for an enormous amount of political contributions, forms the centerpiece of the urban political economy, and houses the vast majority of its residents? No, I do not.

This state, the state born of actually existing capitalism, can only be bent so far. When I was in college, my economics professor, Jamee Moudud, analogized the capitalist state to a stone wrapped in putty. The exterior is highly malleable and can be stretched into different shapes and forms, the contours of which can be profoundly important to our individual and collective lives. But at its core remains the rock of capitalism and all the surplus accumulation and labor exploitation inexorably embedded within it, unchanged and unchangeable from within the system.

The capitalist state cannot fully decommodify housing—a necessary precondition to a right to housing—without replacing this locus of capital accumulation with another stable strategy and thus displacing the site of exploitation from the home to another sphere. The putty's radical reformation cannot reach the center, which remains intact, and is in fact insulated by the surrounding superstructure.

Within the capitalist state, change is possible, up to a point. We can certainly alter the personnel of politics, and that can go a long way toward altering policy, but, as the Greek French sociologist Nicos Poulantzas argued decades ago, "Although the members of the State apparatus belong by their class origin to different classes, they function according to a specific internal unity." This unity of purpose "is no coincidence, it is by reason of the system itself: the direct participation of members of the ruling class in the state apparatus is not the *cause* but the *effect*."[39] In other words, the point of the capitalist state is to reproduce the capitalist political-economy in some form, regardless of the backgrounds and intentions of those who lead and maintain it.

Politicians and parties present various justifications for their reforms' limitations and often point to opposite ideological touchstones to explain policy continuities across administrations. My friend Sylvia Morse identified what we might call "the Richard rule" of twenty-first-century New York City politics: conservative mayor Michael Bloomberg and progressive mayor Bill de Blasio preferred some of the same land-use strategies, but their supporters cited competing ideological justifications. Both administrations pursued a succession of working-class neighborhood upzonings, and, until de Blasio's eighth and final year in office, neither administration used the same approach to increase housing production in wealthy lower-density neighborhoods. Bloomberg's allies justified this pattern and practice with Richard Florida's theory of cultivating the "creative class," while de

Blasio's justified the same course of action by leaning on Richard Rothstein's call to reverse redlining.[40] The Richards come and go, but the policies persist.

With Zohran Mamdani, New York City might be about to experience its first socialist mayor (unless we count David Dinkins, a lapsed DSA member—though he did deliver a mayoral welcome address to the Socialist International convention during his first year in office,[41] or Fiorello La Guardia, who was endorsed by the Socialist Party but never joined its ranks[42]). A mayor like Mamdani could very well turn away from the Richard rule and pursue a radically different policy agenda. But even if he does, it is easy to map out how his agenda could be quashed by forces outside of his control. The state could refuse to raise taxes on the rich, which he has pitched as the means to fund programs like free childcare and buses, and the federal government could withhold the funds the city needs to remain operational. The federal government could also flood the city with secret immigration police, and, when the mayor pushes back, the president could send in the military—as he has already done in Los Angeles and Washington, DC. If this happens, it is not clear that the New York Police Department would side with the DSA mayor over the "law and order" president (who, of course, routinely breaks laws and creates disorder). In addition to initiating a capital strike, the real estate industry could sue to block the mayor's proposed rent freeze, with the hope of ending the system that enables it altogether.

These are just a few of the ways municipal socialism might be blocked, exciting as its prospect may be. The federalist system was designed to quash "factions" and protect both the ability of the majority to subjugate minority groups (when it comes to race) and for the minority to subjugate the majority (when it comes to class). And without a large majority of socialist voters actively supporting a socialist agenda, and not just a plurality of voters opting for the socialist candidate but rejecting the implications of a socialist program, we might find that executive power is less determinative than it appeared from outside the gates of City Hall. As Walter Lippmann wrote in 1913, one year into another New York State experiment with municipal socialism—the Schenectady mayoralty of George Lunn—"The great danger . . . is to have the externals of power and none of its substance."[43]

One can point to counterexamples, like Vienna, as models of the democratic and electoral road to municipal socialism and a right to housing. There, a popular elected government built high-quality mass social housing accessible to a large majority of the population and continues to maintain it to this day. But that road can look much smoother through the gloss of political narrative than its real history should suggest.

True, Vienna's Social Democrats and their social housing system have been extremely popular for a long time. But the party came into power only after a world war toppled the Austro-Hungarian Empire and its monarchy, the country's economy collapsed almost entirely, and a first-ever election was held to usher in a new order. Sixteen years into the Red Vienna project, Austro-Fascists pushed them out and welcomed in the Nazis, initiating some of the worst atrocities in human history. After the Nazis were toppled the Social Democrats managed to rise back to power in Vienna and have remained in office ever since.

The social housing model initiated under Red Vienna was tolerated by capital in large part because it enabled capitalists to keep wages lower than in competitor nations, and because the party largely shifted production from municipal rentals to mortgage-backed nonprofit cooperatives. The Social Democratic Party continues to win elections, and it retains an impressive degree of support and legitimacy in large part through the success of its housing program, but the city's twentieth-century history is not exactly a portrait of parliamentary decorum and peaceful transitions, nor is it an easily replicable model or one without cataclysmic risks.

If the capitalist state is significantly limited in its capacity for self-reform, we might look to other nonstate institutions to help fulfil this role. In the US today, the primary actors we might engage with are labor unions and politicized nonprofits.

For centuries, unions have offered a compelling promise to transform society and have been at the center of syndicalist visions for radical economic democracy. They are the predominant form of organized workers, and they are structurally positioned to challenge capital at the scale of the shop floor, inside the hidden abode of production, as well as at the societal scale. In New York City and beyond, unions have not just defended workers' interests but invested in alternate institutions, from decommodified housing cooperatives to public health clinics. Tenant and housing groups often look to unions for validation and amplification, not only because they see their missions as aligned but also because organized labor can carry an unmatched degree of political power in union-dense cities and states.

These alliances, however, often go only so far. Unless the unions are, like the old Industrial Workers of the World, out to take down the capitalist class as a whole, they will not undermine the economic basis of the industry that hires their members and pays the wages and benefits they have won through organizing, strikes, and collective bargaining. We then see uncomfortable alliances form—not between unions and other working-class actors but between unions and employers, who together fight for public policies that grow revenues and therefore promise both higher profits for business owners and better contracts for unions—sometimes at the expense of the consumer. (In the case of housing, although this language is a bit uncomfortable, "the consumer" is the tenant or the home buyer.)

Building trades unions often catch hell from housing activists and analysts, either for pushing for high-end development projects or for driving up construction costs by using public policy to mandate higher wages. This is not a new phenomenon. In his 1872 pamphlet *The Housing Question*, Friedrich Engels wrote that France's post-Commune planning and building boom aimed not only to make the streets harder for workers to seize, but also "to develop a specifically Bonapartist building trades' proletariat dependent on the government and to turn the city into a pure luxury city."[44] The construction unions might become a dependable partner for mass social housing development under a socialist government, but in the meantime are content to continue to build the luxury city union members could never afford. (A long-ago coworker at the city's building service workers' union shared an old joke with me: A hangman tells a group of workers to build their own gallows. After conferring among themselves, they return to the hangman and ask, "Does it pay union scale?")

Public sector unions can sometimes become partners in housing and tenant struggles, as in the cases of teachers' unions (most notably in Chicago and Los Angeles) that have included housing in their scope, as they recognize that students' living conditions are central to teachers' working conditions. Many public sector unions, however, can be reluctant to challenge mayors and governors who sit on the other side of their collective bargaining tables. More often, they might seek to endorse the executive's questionable housing policies in order to be seen as a reliable partner come contract negotiation time.

As mentioned earlier, US unions' stake in housing and public policy is not just about their current membership and their next contract, but also their pension funds and their future ability to retire in comfort and dignity. If union pensions are wrapped up in real estate, there is a whole other round of stakes attached to the prospects for decommodifying housing and exsecting the profit motive.[45] They might support some degree of affordable housing production, as in the case of the AFL-CIO's Housing Investment Trust, but this program can only go so far before it undermines the entire purpose of their investments, which is to produce a reliable rate of growth far into the future.

All these factors converge to form a dilemma that is, yet again, quite old: unions are at once the primary existing antagonist to capital, and sometimes also to the capitalist state, and yet they are also deeply dependent on the ongoing strength and stability of both. Rosa Luxemburg identified many of these contradictions in her 1906 work *The Mass Strike, the Political Party and the Trade Unions*. As unions grow more active in public policy and market shaping, "we no longer have here a struggle between Labor and Capital, but the solidarity of Capital and Labor against the total consumers."[46] Unions are, she wrote two years later in *Reform or Revolution*, "the organized *defense* of labor power against the attacks of profits," but their attempt to both achieve this goal while also reshaping the labor market in their favor amounts to "a sort of labor of Sisyphus."[47] Unions, then, are indispensable sources of worker power, but they are constrained by their own structural ties with industry and the state from leading a full transformation of something as central to capitalist society as housing and real estate.

In light of these constraints, some on the left turn their hopes toward nonprofits, or what are known in the rest of the world as nongovernmental organizations (NGOs). Nonprofits can take a myriad of forms, from major hospitals and universities that form the backbone of many local economies to small and radical workers' centers and community land trusts. The kinds of nonprofits most relevant to this discussion are those that build affordable housing—community development corporations—and those that organize renters and people enduring homelessness.

Though they have many precursors, today's nonprofit housing developers can mostly trace their roots to the 1960s Great Society programs, the urban disinvestment crises of the late 1960s through the 1980s, and the neoliberal political-economic turn of the mid-1970s and 1980s. With a mix of government, foundation, and corporate funding, these institutions stepped into the structural absence left by capital flight and public sector demobilization and became the leading builders of subsidized housing and the leading advocates for low-income communities.

Many of America's most prominent nonprofit community organizing projects, meanwhile, grew out of the tradition of Saul Alinsky, who, in 1930s Chicago, established a lasting model: hire outside organizers; pull together a geographically determined constituency; mobilize them around discrete campaigns against a common enemy; and seek to extract concessions from governments, banks, corporations, and other powerful actors. The goal was to build community strength, understood more as the ability to influence power than to seize it.

Alinsky died in 1972, but his legacy has lasted. The 1990s saw the rise of a new crop of neo-Alinskyite organizing projects that continue to operate in New York and around the country today. Most are nonprofits, but around the same time they arrived on the scene, many US unions adopted the same playbook, as they shifted focus away from on-site workplace organizing and toward higher-order corporate campaigns.[48]

As a sector, nonprofits are both a response to neoliberalism and an element of it. They often mobilize to oppose public sector rollbacks, but they also stand to fill in the gaps left by government retrenchment using a mix of public- and private-sector revenue streams, thus creating a long-term interdependency between state, capital, and charitable sectors for the provision of basic social goods like housing. Nonprofits rose to prominence in the US under conditions of urban disinvestment, and specifically landlord abandonment and developer disinterest in city centers. They were supposed to build the affordable housing neither the state nor the private developers would, to take over the buildings that landlords were walking away from, and to smooth the path for reinvestment and job growth. Over time, in New York and other cities like it, these conditions have inverted, with nonprofits now situated in capital-saturated real estate markets and forced to retool into organizations competing for space and money against some of the biggest corporations on earth.

The sociologists Nicole Marwell and Paul-Brian McInerney describe this as a five-step cycle that has been repeated in communities across the country.[49] First, nonprofits establish themselves in a disinvested urban neighborhood, often growing out of local organizing efforts. Over time, they expand and formalize their operations, becoming a recognized voice for the community. As they prove their capacity, the government steps back and contracts greater amounts of work to the nonprofit, and corporations invest in the area the nonprofit helped to put back on track, thus raising local land and property values. Next, neighborhood prices rise, and state plans turn toward redevelopment and raising the tax base. Finally, as gentrification takes root and the area is seen as a safe investment, for-profit firms take over the redevelopment process, transforming the nonprofit from a vanguard to a rear-guard force.

Meanwhile, unlike unions, most nonprofits are not funded by member dues and thus must seek out alternative forms of steady income. Some turn directly to corporate sources for support, but most operate on a combination of private foundation and government funding. While this can pay the bills, it also sets up a misalignment between the social forces nonprofits aim to represent and the sources of their ongoing operations. US foundations are, among other things, tax havens for the exceedingly rich. They collect what Ruth Wilson Gilmore has called "twice stolen wealth—(a) profit sheltered from (b) taxes."[50] Nonprofits are not necessarily deferential to the billionaire class, but they do have to watch their backs if they edge close enough to true class conflict. Funding from state sources, meanwhile, often comes with the implicit understanding that the recipient will not directly protest the donor, or else they risk losing any chance of future funding. Whatever their political expression might be, nonprofits must always be careful not to bite the hand that feeds them—at least not *too* hard.

But it is not just funding mechanisms that limit nonprofits' political activities. Perhaps a deeper layer of constraint comes from what a nonprofit can and can't do, at least in this country. Community development corporations and neo-Alinskyite nonprofits generally do not organize workers at the site of production, and so they cannot organize to withhold labor as a means of protest and direct action. They can organize for tenants to withhold their rent, perhaps, or participate in a consumer boycott, but more often they work in the realm of symbolic action. These protests, rallies, and press conferences are primarily designed to attract media attention, which is then meant to put pressure on elected officials, landlords, or other targets. This can be effective, but as US local media withers (and in many parts of the country it has already disappeared altogether), and as nonprofit tactics lose their novelty for the remaining reporters, this strategy can yield diminishing returns.

Those seeking big policy changes might recognize that the current elected official in their district is an obstacle and wish to support a primary campaign against them. This can prove challenging, however, as US tax and election law constrains nonprofits' abilities to engage in this kind of explicit electioneering. Many elected officials understand this to mean that they can appease or ignore nonprofits as they like with little fear of direct political consequences. In these cases, nonprofits become the powerless brokers of the city, afforded a seat at the table but unable to alter the terms of discussion.

In part as a result of their political limitations, many nonprofits focus instead on building various forms of desperately needed affordable housing. To do so, most must rely on the US's uniquely baroque mechanism for funding below-market housing production: the Low-Income Housing Tax Credit. As mentioned previously, rather than direct public funding for the provision of social goods, the federal government produces tax credits and gives them to states, which then award them to nonprofit and for-profit developers, who sell them to tax-dodging investors, all to build housing whose affordability requirements can expire after thirty years. Journalist Alyssa Katz characterized this as "a better-than-nothing gimmick that helps the poor by rewarding the rich," which in the process of producing housing also creates "a vast industry of financial companies in symbiosis with for-profit middlemen and community-based nonprofits."[51] The system is designed to tie the poor's imperative for housing to the rich's desire for tax dodges.

This can leave nonprofits "defang[ed] of oppositional practices and positions," in the words of Cindi Katz.[52] They are a crucial producer and provider of below-market housing for millions of people throughout this country, and yet they are not positioned to transform the housing sector away from being a profit-seeking venture and toward a rights-based regime. While they may not exactly generate profits themselves, they are structurally positioned to not prevent others from making a killing. And so the killing continues.

Although it is not a traditional or central current on the left, there are also those who view developers as progressive elements of capital with the potential to resolve the housing crisis. By expanding production and reducing scarcity and thus building enough housing for everybody as quickly as possible, left YIMBYs hope to construct a market in which home prices contract as availability expands and thus achieve a functional—if not necessarily legal—right to housing.

This agenda has thus far focused on rezoning land to allow higher degrees of residential density. Here it is important to distinguish the dynamics of New York City from most of the rest of the country. While 85 percent of New York City's residentially zoned land allows multifamily buildings or row houses, and much of it enables a mix of residential, commercial, and community uses in buildings and blocks, a staggering 75 percent of residential land in many US cities is zoned for nothing but detached single-family homes.[53] New York can certainly improve its own zoning, but in the US, its land-use code and built environment are outliers.

Clearly, the homeowners' imperative to keep lot sizes large and construction limited to isolated houses is antithetical to a right to housing, makes environmental and transit goals difficult if not impossible to achieve, and makes homes more expensive and neighborhoods more segregated. Exclusionary zoning is not a liberatory policy, and having enough housing for everyone is a definitional component of a universal right to housing.

Furthermore, if a local population is growing—and growing richer, too—as the housing supply stays stagnant, then higher-income residents can up-bid market prices, leading to more gentrification and displacement. (This would also be a reason to institute universal rent control and build social housing, but never mind that for now.)

Sooner or later, however, the pursuit of profit undermines the pursuit of plenitude. A third to half of the financing for new housing construction comes from equity investors, who will only put their money into housing construction if local rents and property values are rising. Once this ceases to be the case, investors turn their dollars to other, faster-growing sectors. At that point, construction slows and little is gained. Of course, public investment could replace the private equity share, and the state could use that leverage to levy rent control and affordability requirements on developers, but that would be a very different model from the one American cities are currently considering.[54]

There can also be other, more chaotic economic effects of a building boom. When land use changes incentivize much more intensive development, they can also drive up the value of land, which is then factored into the price of new housing. As long as land itself is treated as a commodity, and an undertaxed one at that, this cycle can continue.[55] Meanwhile, a sudden and widespread building boom can swell the demand not only for land but also for labor and construction materials, which can cause the cost of both to climb—a boon for contractors and the steel, glass, and timber industries, but not necessarily for would-be renters or buyers.

Of course there is a relationship between supply, demand, and price, and the status quo of scarcity and sprawl is utterly indefensible, but still: multiple supplies and demands interact in a more complex and contradictory fashion than the current debate acknowledges. Ultimately, if the point of the left housing program is to decommodify our homes and remove what should be a right from the vagaries of the market, neither constraining the supply of new housing nor counting on supply alone makes much sense.

Like rental assistance programs, zoning reform and calls for increased development can unite fractions of the political right and left around a common—if limited—program. However, it always flummoxes me when local landlord lobby groups (like the New York Apartment Association) espouse the line that the way to reduce housing costs is to build more private housing, and yet they *also* claim they could not possibly reduce rents in their existing buildings because the amounts their tenants pay today barely keep up with their buildings' maintenance and tax obligations.

These are contradictory claims. If rents are high because of supply constraints, then landlords are admitting that they are exploiting their market power to squeeze tenants into paying more for existing housing, since vacancies are low and tenants have little choice but to pay whatever the owner demands. If rents are high because maintenance costs have inflated, then a rezoning and growth program would do nothing to decrease landlords' costs and could even increase the prices for those very goods by driving up competition for building materials and construction labor. It must be one way or the other: either landlords are charging "economic rents" (or far more than they need to because they control a scarce good), or they are barely scraping by based on the cost of owning and operating a building.

Because they refuse to open their books to public scrutiny, we cannot know for sure which scenario is the case. And yet, they continue to plead two opposite cases, all to avoid the prospects of stricter rent regulation, code enforcement, or competition from public sector developers. In this light, these capitalists do not appear so progressive after all.

The state, the unions, the nonprofits, the developers—no established sector seems capable of delivering the transformative change we clearly need. Because the US lacks a system of proportional representation, "third" parties are, at least at this moment in history, more likely to be vanity projects than serious contenders for power. Sectarian left formations can build disciplined cadres and develop important theories, but they rarely rise to power at any level. At their worst, they point to their own powerlessness as proof of their purity and attack every competing left formation as their proximate enemy, thus confusing onlookers who might otherwise support the cause and plunging movements into self-destructive distraction. Abandoning institutions altogether is no solution, either, since capitalism's defenders dream of a working class bereft of any vehicle for political and cultural organizing.

This leaves only us: the working class, the left, the flawed institutions we have been handed down, and the new institutions we work to create. We do what we do, because what else can we do, and we pray that somehow it will work.

In a positive light, this orientation to politics reminds me of the form of Judaism I grew up in and continue to practice. The emphasis was never on belief in an immaterial spirit. Instead, we focused on learning and on doing: on learning from doing and doing from learning. A great amount of value was placed on maintaining the knowledge and practice, even—or especially—in hard times. When I asked my atheist father why he kept Kosher and went to synagogue every Saturday, his answer was that we exist as a link in a chain stretching back countless generations, and he could not bear to be the one to break it.

This sentiment applies just as well to my religious practice as it does to my political commitments. We exist along a long line of history, stretching back as far as we can find, and we damn well won't be the generation to leave it behind, regardless of—or perhaps because of—the strength of the forces aligned against us. As Ben Morea, cofounder of the Lower East Side collective Up Against the Wall Motherfucker said in a recent interview, taking on the US warfare state at the height of its war on Vietnam "could've overwhelmed us," but instead "we fought them like they were vulnerable."[56] This approach entails not just commitment but also a suspension of disbelief akin to faith. (Morea is avidly anti-religion and deeply spiritual, so I don't mean to co-opt his words into my personal "religious but not spiritual" orientation.)

From a more critical vantage, however, this orientation to politics can leave the left wandering in a wilderness born not only out of weakness but a profound confusion over direction, possibility, plans, and desires. If we cannot envision a plausible path to victory, it is hard to devise a sensible strategy. In other words, if we are not sure where we are going, it is hard to know what steps to take along the way.

From a prison cell in Fascist Italy, Antonio Gramsci—echoing the words of Romain Rolland before him—called on the left to maintain a "pessimism of the intellect, optimism of the will."[57] We should understand that the odds are against us, and that we will have much to overcome, but we should never let our structural analysis slow our drive to overcome this collective station in society, and we should organize and take action with faith in a victorious future. I have found comfort and purpose in this maxim, and I know many others have, too. (A close friend has these words tattooed on his chest.)

A few years ago, however, in the clarity of a Yom Kippur fast, another phrase entered my mind and implanted itself firmly: *nihilism of the intellect, naivety of the will.* This seemed to perfectly describe the crooked posture I had become accustomed to, and it seemed apropos for many others on the left, too.

Nihilism of the intellect, for me, means not so much a belief in the inherent meaninglessness of everything, but rather the collective collapse of any defined end point, and therefore any clear conduit out of the current crises. We hold fast to political principles in the present but lack a plan to conclusively overcome our oppressors. A pervasive confusion clouds our understanding of what concrete form our social and economic order might take, should we somehow find ourselves with the power to implement our politics—any widely held understanding of how society might operate at the micro and macro levels, how this system would survive in a harsh world, and how it could avoid the historical tendency toward first disciplining imperial capital and then dominating the internal proletariat and peasantry, too.

Naivety of the will is what follows as we attempt to change the world without a strong sense of what, exactly, we're bringing about, or, just as importantly, what it would take to win. We understand that our institutions are irreparably cracked, but they are what we have at our disposal and what we have some say over. We can imagine a different set of institutions—a different state, a different party, a different form of worker and community organization—but it is challenging to birth them within the world we continue to live in, and we are unsure how, exactly, they should operate in the world we hope is to come. And so we heedlessly hurl ourselves into the breach, again and again, trying anything, everything, in a desperate push to claw our way out of the present.

"Nihilism of the intellect, naivety of the will" is not a condemnation of this orientation, nor is it a prescription for a proper way to exist in the present conjuncture. It is simply a description of where we find ourselves—myself very much included.

One reason we continue on through the dimness is that sometimes, somehow, it works! We still win important, concrete victories that can change the lives of millions, even if we are unsure how and why we won them or what we must do next.

In my own personal experience in the New York City housing movement, the clearest example of this is found in the 2019 State of New York rent law reforms, known officially as the Housing Stability and Tenant Protection Act. This was a set of reforms so massive and consequential that I sometimes wonder how the hell we won them at all.[58] It achieved, in one bill, much of what the state's tenant movement had been fighting for over the preceding decades of regulatory retrenchment. It precluded most of the means for landlords to remove apartments from rent stabilization. It removed the "vacancy bonus," which rewarded landlords with a 20 percent rent increase whenever a rent-stabilized apartment changed hands, creating enormous incentives for landlords to harass, evict, and churn through tenants. It limited the amount rents could rise based on often dubious improvement cost estimates. It opened rent stabilization to the entire state, allowing smaller cities and towns to opt-in to strong tenant protections. And unlike previous rounds of rent law fights, these victories would not expire after a set term.

I have tried to explain how the movement achieved this major victory over the landlord lobby.[59] Some of it can be attributed to the decades-long slog of organizing that preceded it. Some can be attributed to the post–Occupy Wall Street and Sanders-inspired electoralist turn in New York's left scene, which successfully removed several nominally Democratic lawmakers who caucused with Republicans in order to block bills like this, and to the inclusion of more radical groups (including autonomous tenant unions and the DSA) in the campaign. Some is explained by a more concerted attempt to build a state-wide tenant coalition—a shift from the previous strategy of aligning New York City tenants with New York City unions and instead trying to build tenant power and solidarity across the state.[60]

But there is still plenty that remains unexplained. How did we catch the real estate industry so flat-footed, when they had dominated state legislative sessions previously? Why did our terrible governor, Andrew Cuomo, refuse to heed the industry's panicked plea and veto the bill, after it passed through the legislature, or at least force line-item revisions to the bill via the "chapter amendment" process? Was it a fluke? Is it confirmation that if we keep grinding away, we will—or at least can—win? Is it proof that a perfect campaign yields profound results?

The results have, in fact, been profound. In their first year alone, New York City's housing agency estimates that the new rent laws spared nearly 16,000 apartments from being deregulated and prevented big rent hikes in 37,000 apartments that turned over during the course of that year.[61] It also drove down sales prices and property values for rent-stabilized buildings, forcing banks and buyers to assess the rents apartments currently command, rather than speculate on the bet that, over time, buyers could drive the rents higher and pull the apartments out of rent regulation. In so doing, it has initiated something of a panic among landlords and their defenders, who seek to roll back these laws rather than allow buildings and banks to face foreclosure and insolvency.

It is too soon to tell where this crisis will lead. Will real estate capital be forced to eat the loss? Will its agents get the state to bail them out? Will state and capital collude to make tenants pay for their past gains?

Although localized and particular to my specific interest in housing, achievements like this challenge the prevailing sense that nothing much happens anymore. I certainly understand the sentiment. Reading through history, and particularly revolutionary history, it can feel as if not just the left but the world itself is stuck in a groove. In 1989, Francis Fukuyama asked if we had reached "The End of History?", or a time when the fall of the Soviet Union would answer one of the defining questions of the twentieth century: whether the arc of history was bending toward communism or capitalism.[62] In the wake of the end of the Cold War, Mark Fisher perceived a great pop-cultural resignation, as music and film seemed to become increasingly self-referential and iterative.[63]

Rarely, however, can a society recognize that its stagnation masks a coming cataclysmic change. Alexei Yurchak captures this affect in his book on everyday life and language in late-period Soviet Union: *Everything Was Forever, Until It Was No More*.[64] One cannot read that monograph, with all its retrospective analysis of linguistic patterns and symbolic representations masking a system that had lost its luster, without wondering whether we, too, are living a version of that experience in present-day advanced capitalist liberal democracies like the United States and the United Kingdom.

In my middle-aged lifetime alone, several world-altering upheavals have seemingly changed everything, again and again. To name just a few: the collapse and fall of the Soviet Union; the end of apartheid in South Africa; the tech booms and busts; the 2001 attacks on the World Trade Center and the Pentagon and the subsequent "global war on terror," including the US wars on Afghanistan and Iraq; the 2008 global financial crisis; the Arab Spring, Occupy Wall Street, and the global movement of the squares; COVID-19, and the still-unfamiliar world left in its wake; Russia's invasion of Ukraine, twice; the rise of a nationalist international, with far-right governments in power in the US and in many nations of the Global North and South; several massive wildfires, droughts, floods, and famines; the ongoing occupation of Palestine, punctuated by two intifadas, the Great March of Return, Hamas's atrocities on October 7, 2023, and Israel's genocidal campaign of extermination and expansion.

Another oft-quoted Gramsci line fits the bill: "The crisis consists precisely of the fact that the old is dying and the new cannot be born; in this interregnum a great variety of morbid symptoms appear."[65] And appear. And appear. This passage increasingly seems to apply not only to "these days" but to all the days of my life—a very long interregnum, indeed.

Clearly this is not a world in which nothing ever happens. Perhaps it is a world in which nothing is ever resolved. In the past ten years alone the world has caught fire several times, sometimes literally. But who, in the words of the labor anthem "Solidarity Forever," can "bring to birth a new world from the ashes of the old"?[66] While we on the left aspire and organize to be the ones to do so, it is largely the right—or perhaps the "diagnolists," who pull together a chaotic, conspiratorial worldview from elements of both the right and the left—which is gaining ground.[67]

It used to be the right who "stands athwart history, yelling Stop," but as the world spins in strange and hostile directions, I sense a temptation from the left to mount this position—though not yet to unabashedly claim the mantle as our own.[68] In 1940, Walter Benjamin theorized that revolution, contrary to Marx's metaphor of "the locomotive of world history," is instead the intervention of the train's passengers, who sense history is careening toward terror and "pull the emergency brake."[69] On the kinds of bad days the world seems to be delivering with great regularity, it feels to me less like we are on the moving train of history and more like we are tied to the tracks as history barrels down at us.

During his campaigns and his presidency, Barack

Obama and his allies frequently mobilized an ontological Martin Luther King quote: "The arc of the moral universe is long, but it bends toward justice." Obama often altered it slightly and presented it as "the arc of *history* is long, but it bends toward justice." They used this phrase both to celebrate wins and to urge patience in the face of defeats, conveying to their audiences that while it takes time and there are setbacks, progress is all but promised. This message, however, was hard to maintain. During a 2015 appearance on *The Daily Show* during the press tour for his book *Between the World and Me*, Ta-Nehisi Coates mused instead that the arc "bends toward chaos."[70] Things get better, and they get worse, but there is no surefire directionality or plan.

Indeed, there is no arc of history, other than what we interpret it to be. The very perception of a historical arc is, like sunrise and sunset, a conceptualization of the dynamics of time and space shaped by our positionality on this earth. We age and we experience history, and it is passed on to us through oral and written traditions. This can create the contours of a plot, a way to turn time into a trajectory toward some greater purpose. But that purpose may not exist, and that trajectory may be nothing more than an accretion of rotations. This is not to say that there is no history, but rather that, as my historian father used to say (paraphrasing Hegel, though I did not know it at the time), "The only thing history teaches is that no one learns from history."

This aimlessness of history, the feeling that the world is barreling toward destruction and yet simultaneously stuck in its ways, seems to be producing on both the left and the right a renewed desire for an immediate and final confrontation to break this impasse—though that finality never seems to arrive. Apocalypse preppers stock bunkers, either shambolic or lavish depending on the particular prepper's class positionality. Pundits predict civil war and chart scenarios for the second great disunion. Christian nationalists and esoteric spiritualists welcome the coming rapture and stoke geopolitical horror as a means to this end. Lubavitchers parade down city streets in Elon Musk's Cybertrucks crying out, "Moshiach now!"

On May Day 2021, I went to a Times Square rally that was primarily focused on New York City's recently unionized Amazon warehouse workers. There were rank-and-file members and recently elected union leaders, along with a smattering of journalists. Most likely because of the timing—COVID vaccines had only recently been released, and the world was still coming out of its shell—there were not a lot of supporters there. The largest group was the Communist Party USA, and particularly their Young Communist League, some of whom had worked as salts in a Staten Island Amazon plant. I remember sitting on a half-wall by the TKTS staircase and watching these Communist youths amassing, waving oversized red banners, and confronting the police. One shouted at a cop, "Your kids will live under our flag!" Their words deteriorated into necrophiliac taunts I will not repeat here, but I was stunned by this young cadre's confidence, their seemingly unshaken belief in the coming red dawn, their pure faith in the inevitable and imminent transformation of capitalism into communism, not only within our lifetimes but any moment, *now*. It was revolutionary cosplay, but I could not tell if they were in on the game. (Who knows, maybe they're right! If it should come to pass, please, comrades, have mercy on me.)

I recalled these Communist kids a couple of years later when I saw a production of Samuel Hunter's play *A Bright New Boise*. It begins with the main character, Will, standing still, staring directly into the audience, saying "Now. Now. Now. Now." Over time, we learn that the protagonist recently exited an extremist Christian sect after one of its members died. He is working at an Idaho Hobby Lobby in the hopes of finding and reconnecting with his estranged teenage son. Over the course of the play, he repeats his incantation of nowness twice more—once more as explanation, and finally as plea.

In the explanatory passage, Will, recalling his deceased friend, says:

> The last time I saw Danny, we hid in the Albertsons until everyone had left and then we went out into the parking lot, and we prayed for Christ to come again. We prayed for all of it to go away, we prayed for all of it to be swallowed up in divine fire, every disgusting house and parking lot and interstate and car and person on fire turning into ash and reforming as a city of pure light that was brilliant and eternal and

> unchanging and we prayed dear Jesus now. Now. Now. Now. And then nothing happened.

Near the close of the play, in a moment of panic and indecision, Will reverts to this mantra again, shouting eight times, "Now." "It never works," his son finally says.[71]

From revolutionary Communists to end-times Christians, it seemed, everyone was crying NOW into the wind, summoning some deliverance from a reality they disown but cannot escape, as if the very act of declaring it done would cast a spell over this fallen world and bring about the new one. Sometimes, particularly at rallies decrying homelessness, even chanting "Fight! Fight! Fight! Housing is a human right!" can make me feel a bit like Hunter's character, invoking the harried mantra of "now" to no end.

Meanwhile, as the frustrated drive toward a final confrontation percolates through our politics, a dialectically opposed orientation to the stubborn present is manifesting in our popular culture. Our books and films have lately been filled with stories based on the multiverse, or the concept that every personal decision produces a split in space-time and a parallel counter-reality in which one decides otherwise. This creates a proliferation of universes, some fairly similar to the one we know and others dramatically different.

This narrative form can open up a world of radical and infinite possibility, in which the strictures of our society collapse and suddenly anything imaginable is real. The title of one of the most successful multiverse parables conveys this promise: *Everything Everywhere All at Once*. In one sense, this is an absolute rejection of Margaret Thatcher's mantra of neoliberalism: "There is no alternative." *Au contraire*, the multiverse narrative parries; there is nothing *but* alternatives.

But there is something about the multiverse plot that can be distinctly neoliberal. Its alternatives are not won through collective struggle. They are not the outcome of political contests, of organizing, or of historical necessity. Fear not, the form suggests: nothing needs to be changed in the world we know, because it is but one of infinite worlds. If we are suffering in this one, another version of ourselves flourishes elsewhere. The factor that produces these divergent pathways is not persuasion or conquest, but rather *individual choice*—a cornerstone of neoliberal ideology, as Ujju Aggarwal argues in her book *Unsettling Choice*.[72] Everything—literally everything—rides on our solitary selections. While the phrase "everything everywhere all at once" may negate one of Thatcher's famous utterances, the structure of the metaverse narrative calls to mind another: "There's no such thing as society. There are individual men and women and there are families."[73] Our individual and familiar agency, this narrative structure implies, determines the course of everything.

It seems many of us have lost—or have been alienated from—any shared faith in a dramatically better future we could collectively create. This is not just an issue for the left; in recent years, both anarchist anthropologist David Graeber and reactionary technologist Peter Thiel have expressed their disappointment in the fact that the hovercrafts they were promised as children never materialized, and instead all we got were tweets.[74]

My own political faith has been shaken not only by the worsening state of the world but by an overdue reckoning with my own left traditions. A few years ago I read Vivian Gornick's *The*

Romance of American Communism, a beautiful tribute to the affective dimensions of radical politics but also an outpouring of grief and rage over the betrayal of American Communists' belief in the party and the world it promised.[75] I went on to read Max Elbaum's *Revolution in the Air*, which dives into the largely forgotten world of the New Communist Movement of the 1970s and '80s (and went a long way toward explaining the resume gap in many of my mentors' self-narrative), but also displays the depths of pettiness and factionalism that take hold when the coming insurrection never arrives.[76] Next was M. Gessen's *Where the Jews Aren't*, a short history of the Jewish autonomous zone in the Soviet Union, Birobidzhan, which promised a classless society in which Yiddish culture could flourish and reach its full potential, but ultimately delivered persecution, censorship, show trials, and executions.[77]

The work that really pulled the ground out from under me was Bini Adamczak's *Yesterday's Tomorrow*, which charts the Soviet Union's turn against its own partisans, told backward, starting with train cars of Jews and antifascists being hauled to Nazi Germany and ending at the crushing of the Kronstadt rebellion with the backing of not just the worst villains of Soviet history but also Lenin, Trotsky, and even Alexandra Kollontai. Beyond detailing these compounding crimes, Adamczak conveys the world destruction they represented for believers. The betrayals of the Soviet Union not only corrupted the Marxist left's faith in a specific party and program, but in the future itself. The party and the future were one and the same, and then they were gone.

Reading this book, I realized that I still carried a sentimental attachment to the promised but undelivered future, even if I had no party to attach it to—a vestigial messianism that was already assured and despoiled well before I was born. To lose this entirely is to live in time without teleology, to give up on the idea that tomorrow must improve on today. "Utopia lost," Adamczak writes. "This strange, wispy phrase, which sounds rather like the title of a conference of theologians, means quite simply that today, the greater part of the future already lies behind us."[78]

If the future lies behind us, the past lies beneath us. In a commentary for *Jewish Currents* on the bitter portion of Torah known as Naso, Raphael Magarik reflected on the Situationist slogan "under the pavement, the beach!" and insisted that not just a carnival lies below but also an endless substratum of history, pain, struggle, and suppression. "Awaiting us there is not a hippy paradise, but a genizah of past traumas, social worlds forcibly remade by new elites, revolutions accidentally unleashed and violently put down."[79]

All of this can make our contemporary struggles for things like a right to housing in twenty-first-century New York City seem somewhat quixotic. What, exactly, is possible, and what is not? It is hard to say. Two friends, both prominent fixtures in the New York housing movement, recently got into a joking argument about which of them had the more far-fetched belief system: Was it the one who was working toward a communist revolution in the heart of the global hegemon, or the one seeking municipal social democracy in the command center of the global financial system?

We are working tirelessly toward decommodifying housing in New York, and while we attempt to move the needle and build up a parallel social housing system that stands as a bulwark against the reign of private property, we are all well aware that it is difficult—if not impossible—to achieve this outcome in full.

First, public development under capitalism still relies on private profit: the state extracts a social wage from surplus, but without ongoing profits—and thus without ongoing exploitation—construction cranes stand still. Organized popular power can push capital and the state into a social democratic compact, but such an order is still endogenous to capitalism, and thus relies on both continued growth and continued cooperation from capital—neither of which, these days, seems too safe a bet.[80]

Second, decommodification is not a one-time commitment, but an ongoing project that requires not only sustained political support but ongoing subsidy. The two, in fact, are closely linked. Too often, social housing gets built and forgotten, allowing conditions to deteriorate in ways that undermine not only the lives of residents but faith in the project altogether. If the housing system and budgets do not allow for ongoing maintenance and systemic improvements, the system will fail on both economic and social grounds.

Third, to fully decommodify a core economic element, we would also need to decommodify its key components. In the case of housing, that would mean addressing not just raw materials like glass and steel, difficult as that would be, but also—and more consequentially—the very building blocks of housing and society as a whole: land and labor. Once we are talking about decommodifying land and labor, we are not talking about an ambitious policy agenda but rather a revolution. Are we ready to take these implications seriously? If so, how? If not, at what cost?

Inaction is out of the question. The status quo is untenable, with hundreds of thousands homeless while hundreds of thousands earn millions each year. Mainstream conservative and liberal ideas on housing are culs-de-sac that only lead back to the conditions we contend with today.

Under these circumstances, one could easily descend into the worst versions of left-wing melancholy, a tendency Walter Benjamin identified a century ago as a perennial trap for depressive leftists who take more comfort in nursing the wounds of past defeats than in forging new political programs in the present. The left-wing melancholic "takes as much pride in the traces of former spiritual goods as the bourgeois do in their material goods" and holds an "attitude to which there is no longer in general any corresponding political action," preferring instead "negativistic quiet."[81]

Benjamin was famously saturnine himself, and perhaps his polemic against this type was in part an attempt to steel himself against its lure. More recently, Enzo Traverso has written in defense of left melancholy, arguing that we live in the "eclipse of utopias," a shattered mirror world in which the cracked reflection of our historical defeat is inescapably present.[82] We can criticize the feeling, but it is not so easy to excise it. It may be as much a part of us as the will to move beyond it.

I remember writing, at the end of the introduction to my book *Capital City*, "I believe that we will win." I was excited by that phrase, which oddly originated at the US Naval Academy Preparatory School and then became popular at US sporting events before migrating to Black Lives Matter and other protests, all of its pithy confidence intact. In both contexts it is chanted as a compounding call and response: "I *I!* I believe. *I believe!* I believe that we will win. *I believe that we will win!*" Then I was willing myself to believe; now it is harder to do so with the full confidence of my convictions.

I am not trying to be edgy or cool. This is not a call for quietude or a retreat into the warm wet blanket of complacent gloom. I am just being honest.

I know that I am supposed to end an address like this with an appeal to hope, but why? How many lectures have you heard or books have you read where the speaker or author spends four-fifths of their time on the structural reasons why things are so screwed up, only to appeal in the final passages to some fix, be it an underwhelming policy reform or a revolution that arises out of thin air? Too many works pitched to activists promise that "when we fight, we win," which sounds encouraging to the author but can read as taunting to those of us fighting everyday yet winning few battles. "You are just not fighting hard enough," these works seem to imply—a message I would not want to send to an audience of overworked organizers.

Last year I was on a panel following a series of short documentaries about New York City housing struggles. For the closing question, the moderator, my friend Betty Yu, asked what gives us hope. "Oh no," I thought to myself. Feeling a flash of panic at how to respond both candidly and appropriately, I recalled Mariame Kaba's famous exhortation: "Hope is a discipline."[83] I fully agree, I thought to myself, but failing that, so is persistence despite hopelessness.

Tragically first in line, I gave the answer no one was looking for. "I have no hope," I said, which drew gasps from the audience—the only time I can remember ever eliciting that kind of response. "But every day," I continued, "I get up and do what needs to be done, regardless." It is entirely sensible to be hopeless, but it is entirely senseless to give up.

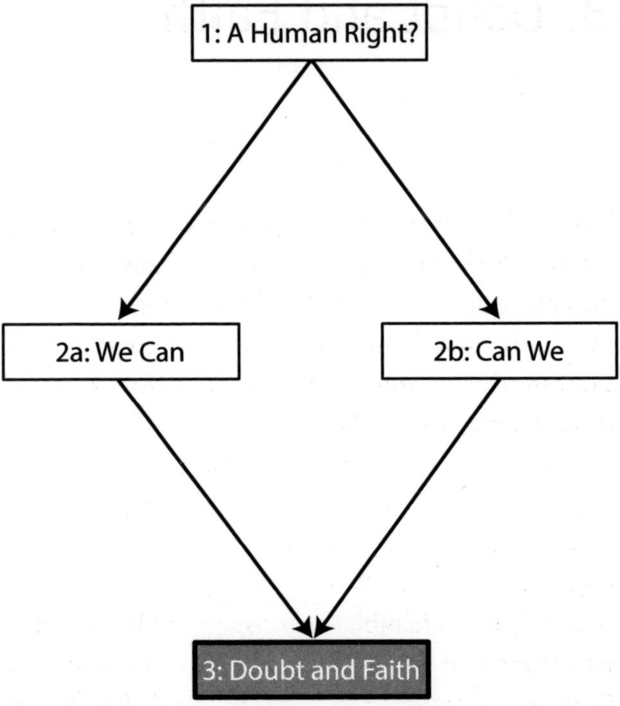
1: A Human Right?
2a: We Can
2b: Can We
3: Doubt and Faith

3. Doubt and Faith

I will close with two lessons from my recent rabbis. Neither teaching directly answers the housing question, if such a thing is even possible, but both model the orientation we must maintain in this moment, as the question lingers, festers, and ultimately explodes.

I never left Judaism (and I don't believe I ever could, even if I wanted to), but I've resumed a more regular religious practice over the past five years—essentially since COVID. Returning to religion is probably a predictable response to the horror of a pandemic and the solitude required to combat it. Certainly logging in to a radical Rosh Hashanah service with thousands of congregants felt liberating after months of isolation, similar to the feeling of joining in mass (and masked) protests during the George Floyd rebellion a few months prior.

But as much as a new community, I was seeking a new vantage—another way to take in the vast space between the broken world we inhabit and the better world we envision. I could not keep returning to the same old sources to explain the ways of the world. Much the way many leftists seemed to take a new interest in psychoanalysis during this moment of isolation and insularity, I wanted to see what it might look like to observe the world through the lens of several thousands of years of Jewish thought and practice. No need to leave Marx behind, but he could make room for other rabbis.

I found a home at Kolot Chayeinu, a radical egalitarian congregation about an hour away from my home—a schlep, to be sure, but a worthy one. Their mission statement is emphatically ambiguous, proclaiming that "doubt can be an act of faith," and their services feature not only lessons from the rabbinate but sermons by the congregants, who use Jewish texts and commentary to make sense of this undoing world.

As much as I was inspired by the lay leaders' wisdom, I was also pulled in by the rabbi at the time, Miriam Grossman. I had known Rabbi Grossman (who is almost universally known in the community as "Rabbi Miriam," but I choose to be more formal here) as a supporter of a litany of left-wing causes, from Indigenous and Palestinian solidarity to racial equality and labor rights. I had probably chanted the words "Fight! Fight! Fight! Housing is a human right!" along with her a dozen times before I set foot in her synagogue (which is actually located in a Presbyterian church that rents its space to our congregation). As an activist, Rabbi Grossman brought a strong moral conviction to our shared political commitments. But as a congregational leader, she mixed that same political compass with a remarkable vulnerability, including a willingness to candidly admit that she did not always know what to do, think, or say.

As the congregation recovered from the pandemic, Rabbi Grossman announced that she would be departing from the synagogue and seeking out other opportunities away from the pulpit. We were all sad to see her go. She announced several months in advance that her last service would be one week after the joyous holiday of Simchas Torah—that is, on October 14, 2023.

The week before was one of those dates that becomes a stand-in for what we understood to have happened. I have lived through at least three of these in my adult life: September 11, January 6, October 7. Just one week later, the congregation was shaken by the scale of violence that had already befallen the peoples between the river and the sea, and all the more horror that was clearly coming for Gaza—a horror we were committed to stopping with all the power we could summon.

On October 14, the synagogue was packed. I arrived early but was still shuffled up to the standing-room section of the balcony. There was a thick tension in the air. The cantor, Lisa B. Segal, altered several of the melodies to match the mournful moment, including a version of the normally ecstatic Psalm 150 set to the searching tune of Leonard Cohen's "Hallelujah."

When it came time for her sermon, Rabbi Grossman began by returning to the address I had heard her deliver a month prior on Yom Kippur, which called on us to commit to climate action with all that we had.[1] That sermon closed, "I want to leave you with this: do not give up." On this day, she needed to hear her own words again because, she confessed, "I don't have hope today."

This hit hard. It is not what you are supposed to say, but it was clearly true, for Rabbi Grossman and likely for many of those assembled. Certainly, it was true for me.

"Fine," she continued. "I don't have hope today. But maybe I don't need hope today." Rabbi Grossman went on to list all the immediate actions she would be taking, despair be damned, ranging from personal acts of compassion and condolence to political acts of courage and commitment. "Today I need to say apartheid and occupation ultimately does not keep anyone safe. Today I need to say war crimes do not justify war crimes. Today I need to keep my humanity. And today I need to keep going even without hope. Because hope will come one day."

Rather than conjure hope out of hopelessness, she would instead "prepare her a beautiful room" and "lure her towards me. I set the table for her arrival through action, through not turning away." One day, hope may return, and if she does, we will be ready to greet her because we never stopped acting in her absence. In the meantime, we will care for one another and we will fight for what we believe in, equally liberated and alienated from all assurances.

Following this service, our congregation hosted a slew of interim Rabbis to lead us as we searched for a new permanent teacher. One of them was Rabbi Abby Stein (no relation to me and known more commonly among congregants as Rabbi Abby). She is probably more comfortable behind barricades than pulpits, but she made a temporary exception to help us in our transitional time.

Rabbi Stein, too, was familiar to me from the New York left. She is particularly committed to housing struggles because of her own experiences with housing precarity. She grew up in Brooklyn's Satmar Hassidic community and comes from a long lineage of respected rabbis, going all the way back to the legendary founder of Hasidism, the Baal Shem Tov. When Rabbi Stein came out to her family as trans, however, she was shunned and struggled with homelessness. In addition to fighting for trans rights, women's rights, Palestinian rights, and more, she has been a strong supporter of the tenant and homeless movements in New York and beyond.

When Hanukkah 2024 rolled around, Rabbi Stein encouraged our synagogue not to downplay the holiday. For most American Jews,

Hanukkah is not all that religiously significant, in contrast with the "high holidays" of Rosh Hashanah and Yom Kippur. In retrospect, the story's heroes may not seem entirely heroic. But in her own Hassidic upbringing, Hanukkah remained an important observance, with some scholars insisting that it is one of the *most* essential holidays. (Granted, for every holiday, one can find a Jewish scholar who argues that it is, in fact, the holiest.)

Rabbi Stein recounted her yeshivah training to draw lessons from the Hanukkah story, and particularly the seemingly minor miracle of the holiday. Advancing Jewish guerillas arrived at their holy temple and rid it of Greek religious paraphernalia. In the course of cleaning up, they found one small, ritually sealed container of oil. It would take another eight days to procure more. The oil they found should have only been enough to illuminate the space for one night, but somehow its flames burned for eight.

The miracle in question had always been explained to me as God extending the life of the light for seven extra days. True, Rabbi Stein said, but emphasizing God's relatively mundane intervention misses the point entirely.

The miracle, she taught, is not that God extended the lamp's life; the miracle is that our (real or fictional) ancestors lit it anyway, without any cause to believe that it would last. They had no foreknowledge or guarantees of what was to come, no sense of how their war-weary present might proceed into a peaceful future. God intervened not because they believed, necessarily, but rather because, in a moment of helplessness, they acted nonetheless. The power exists entirely in the determination, not in the deliverance.

Acknowledgments

This book is dedicated to my mother, Penney Stein, who instilled in me a love and respect for land and books. She also kindly volunteered to copyedit the proof along with me, overcoming my reluctance by arguing irrefutably that it would be better for her to find the mistakes before publication than afterward. I am forever grateful.

I am thankful to my wife, Sarah Ema Friedland, for her love and support during the development of this book, and always.

My thanks go out to those who initially invited me to participate in a gathering on the right to housing in New York City: Karen Kubey, Gabriella Rendon, and Miguel Robles-Duran. Thanks also to Deborah Gans for offering an incisive counterpoint to my address. Portions of this book were delivered at their event on

October 9, 2025, held at the Parsons Housing Justice Lab.

Thank you to my editor, Leo Hollis, for embracing this unconventional concept and improving it markedly. Thanks also to Bruno George for copyediting and fact-checking, and to Tim Thomas for getting this book out into the world.

A few sections are summaries of arguments I made and histories I told in my doctoral dissertation. Thank you to my brilliant advisor, Cindi Katz, for all her mentorship and inspiration, both during that time and in the years since, and to each member of my stellar dissertation committee: Tom Angotti, Ruth Wilson Gilmore, and Ian MacDonald.

Because this book is a "speculative speech" and is meant to mimic my speaking style, many of its thoughts and phrases were first uttered in discussions with friends over the past year or so. Those exchanges sparked and clarified the ideas in this book and offered important challenges to some of my first instincts. I am therefore deeply indebted to conversations with, among many others, L. Israh Afridi, Hadar Ahuvia, Jenny Akchin, Andy Battle, Kenton Card, Marika Dias,

Tom Delgado, Charlie Dulik, Avi Garelick, Zoltan Gluck, Eric Goldfischer, David Greenberg, Eliot Hetterly, Celeste Hornbach, Ryan Joseph, Nancy Lane Kaplan, Cindi Katz, John Krinsky, Mark Krotov, Joe Loonam, Monxo Lopez, Manissa Maharawal, Oksana Mironova, Sylvia Morse, Michael Nicholas, Zach Paganini, Dania Rajendra, Rob Robinson, Zara Serabian-Arthur, Susanne Schindler, Andrew Schustek, Jay Sterrenberg, Nathan Storey, Steve Theberge, Iziah Thompson, Jacob Udell, Ellen Varady, Cea Weaver, Hilary Wilson, and Rami Younis. Special thanks to the Anarcho-Nihilist Book Club and the Judeo-Goyishe Affinity Group for offering feedback on a draft manuscript.

Thank you to my Jewish communities and institutions: Kolot Chayeinu, Jews for Racial and Economic Justice, Jewish Voice for Peace, IfNotNow, *Jewish Currents*, YIVO, Yiddish New York, KlezCummington, and more.

Finally, thank you to New York's housing movement and all its component coalitions, organizations, and members. I hope this book feels more cathartic than disheartening. That was certainly the intention. See you at the next meeting.

Notes

1. A Human Right?

1 Coalition for the Homeless, "How Many People Are Homeless in NYC Altogether?"

2 The US Department of Housing and Urban Development, Office of Community Planning and Development, *The 2024 Annual Homelessness Assessment Report (AHAR) to Congress*, December 2024.

3 Chris Lester, "Homelessness in America: 40 Years of Crisis," *The Flaw*, December 23, 2024.

4 Edward G. Goetz, *New Deal Ruins: Race, Economic Justice, and Public Housing Policy*, Cornell University Press, 2013.

5 Franklin D. Roosevelt, "State of the Union Message to Congress," January 11, 1944.

6 Housing Act of 1949, Public Law 171, Chapter 338, 81st Congress.

7 Gail Radford, *Modern Housing for America: Policy Struggles in the New Deal Era*, University of Chicago Press, 2008, p. 86

8 Radford, *Modern Housing*, p. 185.

9 Juan González, *Reclaiming Gotham: Bill de Blasio and the Movement to End America's Tale of Two Cities*, The New Press, 2017, p. 58.

10 Radford, *Modern Housing*, p. 115

11 Keeanga-Yamahtta Taylor, *Race for Profit: How Banks and the Real Estate Industry Undermined Black Homeownership*, University of North Carolina Press, 2019, p. 37.

12 A. Philip Randolph Institute, *A "Freedom Budget" for All Americans: A Summary,* January 1967.

13 "Bayard Rustin Residence," NYC LGBT Historic Sites Project, nyclgbtsites.org.

14 "Penn South Cooperators in the U.S. Civil Rights Movement," Penn South Coop, pennsouth.coop.

15 Zachary Levenson, *Delivery as Dispossession: Land Occupation and Eviction in the Postapartheid City*, Oxford University Press, 2022.

16 Fran Quigley, "Six Reasons Why Housing Is a Human Right," *Shelterforce,* March 25, 2025.

17 Dick Cluster and the Institute for Policy Studies Working Group on Housing, *The Right to Housing: A Blueprint for Housing the Nation*, Institute for Policy Studies, 1989.

18 Rachel G. Bratt, Michael E. Stone, and Chester W. Hartman, eds., *A Right to Housing: Foundation for a New Social Agenda*, Temple University Press, 2006.

19 Jessica Katz and Robert Robinson, "Taking 'Housing Is a Human Right' from Slogan to Reality," *Gotham Gazette,* July 31, 2021.

2a. We Can

1 Ian Frazier, "Hidden City," *The New Yorker,* October 28, 2013.

2 Coalition for the Homeless, "The Callahan Legacy: Callahan v. Carey and the Legal Right to Shelter."

3 Karen Yi, "New York Opens First-in-Nation Homeless Shelter for Transgender People," *Gothamist,* August 5, 2025.

4 Thomas P. DiNapoli, *New Yorkers in Need: Homelessness in New York State*, Office of the New York State Comptroller, January 2025.

5 New York City Mayors' Management Report, 2025, *Department of Homeless Services*.

6 Coalition for the Homeless, "Basic Facts About Homelessness: New York City."

7 Karen Yi, "It's Harder for Homeless Families Without Young Kids to Get Shelter Beds, Data Shows," *Gothamist,* July 26, 2024.

8 Coalition for the Homeless, "Basic Facts About Homelessness: New York City."

9 Mark Lester, "Eradicating Homelessness in Finland," HUD *PD&R Edge,* July 11, 2023.

10 Marybeth Shinn and Jill Khadduri, "How Finland Ended Homelessness," *Cityscape* 22, no. 2 (2020): 75–80.

11 Jade Vasquez and Celeste Hornbach, *Housing First: A Proven Approach to Dramatically Reduce Street Homelessness,* The Office of the New York City Comptroller, June 2023.

12 Taylor, *Race for Profit*.

13 Cassim Shepard, "Mass Support," *Places Journal*, April 2023.

14 Elle Hunt, "City with a Female Face: How Modern Vienna Was Shaped by Women," *Guardian*, May 14, 2019.
15 Daniel Aldana Cohen, Aaryaman "Sunny" Singhal, Ruthy Gourevitch, and Gianpaolo Baiocchi, *Green Social Housing: Lessons from Vienna*, Climate and Community Institute, June 2025.
16 Michal Kalecki, "Political Aspects of Full Employment," in *The Political Economy: Readings in the Politics and Economics of American Public Policy*, Routledge, 2021, pp. 27–31.
17 Fiscal Policy Institute, "Who is Leaving New York State? Part I: Income Trends" December 5, 2023.
18 Fiscal Policy Institute, "Who is Leaving New York State? Part II: Social Characteristics," June 3, 2024.
19 Henri Lefebvre, *Writings on Cities*, trans. Eleonore Kofman and Elizabeth Lebas, Blackwell, 1996, p. 179.
20 Melinda Cooper, *Counterrevolution: Extravagance and Austerity in Public Finance*, Princeton University Press, 2024.
21 Kafui A. Attoh, "What Kind of Right Is the Right to the City?," *Progress in Human Geography* 35, no. 5 (October 2011): pp. 669.
22 Kelly Anderson "Whose Right, to What City?" *Progressive City*, July 2, 2018.
23 Antonis Vradis, "Intervention – The Right Against the City," *Antipode Foundation,* October 1, 2012.
24 Ipsita Chatterjee, *Displacement, Revolution, and the New Urban Condition: Theories and Case Studies*, SAGE, 2014, p. 8.
25 Samuel Stein, "Their Right to the City, and Ours," *TOPOS*, no. 115 (2021).
26 Frances Fox Piven and Richard Cloward, *Poor People's Movements: Why They Succeed, How They Fail*, Vintage, 1978.

27 Christopher Herbert, Alexander Hermann, and Daniel McCue, "Measuring Housing Affordability: Assessing the 30 Percent Income Standard," Joint Center on Housing Studies of Harvard University, September 2018.

28 Patrick Spauster, "NYC Voucher Households Are Concentrated in a Handful of Neighborhoods, Data Shows," *City Limits,* February 5, 2025.

29 New York City Housing Authority, "Resident Data Book Summary."

30 Shelby R. King, "What If Vouchers Aren't the (Only) Answer?," *Shelterforce*, February 18, 2022.

31 Susanne Schindler and Samuel Stein, "What Makes Rent 'Fair?,' " *Shelterforce,* February 28, 2025.

32 Samuel Stein and Oksana Mironova, "AMI in NYC: Visualizing Inequality and Unaffordability with Area Median Income," *Community Service Society,* May 2024.

33 Sheera Frenkel, "Israel Secretly Targets U.S. Lawmakers with Influence Campaign on Gaza War," *New York Times,* June 5, 2024.

34 *2023 New York City Housing and Vacancy Survey*, US Census Bureau, nyc.gov.

35 Ibid.

36 Oksana Mironova and Tom Waters, "How Social Is That Housing?," *Community Service Society,* February 18, 2020, cssny.org.

37 Gianpaolo Baiocchi and H. Jacob Carlson, "Social Housing 2.0: Viable Non-Market Tools for Today's Housing Crisis," *Urban Democracy Lab at New York University,* April 20, 2022.

38 Amanda Huron, *Carving Out the Commons: Tenant Organizing and Housing Cooperatives in Washington, DC*, University of Minnesota Press, 2018.

39 Suleiman Osman, " 'We're Doing It Ourselves': The

Unexpected Origins of New York City's Public–Private Parks During the 1970s Fiscal Crisis," *Journal of Planning History* 16, no. 2 (2017): 162–74.

40 Benjamin Holtzman, *The Long Crisis: New York City and the Path to Neoliberalism*, Oxford University Press, 2021.

41 Sharryn Kasmir, *The Myth of Mondragón: Cooperatives, Politics, and Working Class Life in a Basque Town*, SUNY Press, 1996.

42 Jacob Udell, Celeste Hornbach, Oksana Mironova, and Samuel Stein, "Social Housing and Housing Justice: Pathways to Housing Decommodification," *Law and Political Economy Project*, May 31, 2022.

43 New York City Housing Authority, "NYCHA FACT SHEET, 2025," nyc.gov.

44 "Subsidized Housing: Across-City Comparison," NYU Furman Center, May 2012, furmancenter.org.

45 New York City Housing Authority, "NYCHA FACT SHEET, 2025," nyc.gov.

46 Joel Schwartz, *The New York Approach: Robert Moses, Urban Liberals, and Redevelopment of the Inner City*, Ohio State University Press, 1993.

47 Manhattan Community Board 11, "Statement of Community District Needs and Community Board Budget Requests," Fiscal Year 2026.

48 Owen Hatherley, *Walking the Streets/Walking the Projects: Adventures in Social Democracy in NYC and DC*, Repeater Books, 2024.

49 New York City Housing Authority, 2024.

50 Stanley Aronowitz, *The Death and Life of American Labor: Towards a New Workers' Movement*, Verso, 2014, p. 149. Joshua Freeman, *Working-Class New York: Life and Labor Since World War II*, The New Press, 2000, pp. 119–20; Anthony Schuman, "Labor and Housing in New

York City: Architect Herman Jessor and the Cooperative Housing Movement," 2005, p. 2; Gail Radford, *Modern Housing for America: Policy Struggles in the New Deal Era*, University of Chicago Press, 2008, p. 18; Hilary Botein, "Labor Unions and Affordable Housing: An Uneasy Relationship," *Urban Affairs Review* 42, no. 6 (2007): 799–822; Walter Mankoff, "A Strategic Alliance: The Story of How Penn South Was Created," *Penn South 50th Anniversary Journal*, (2012), in the author's possession, emailed by Mankoff.

51 Hilary Botein, "Visions of Community: Post-War Housing Projects of Local 3, International Brotherhood of Electrical Workers, and Local 1199, Hospital Workers Union," *Planning Perspectives* 24, no. 2 (2009): 175–96.

52 Jennifer Baum, *Just City: Growing Up on the Upper West Side When Housing Was a Human Right*, Fordham University Press, 2024.

53 Jonathan Tarleton, *Homes for Living: The Fight for Social Housing and a New American Commons*, Beacon Press, 2025.

54 Francesca Mari, "Imagine a Renters' Utopia. It Might Look Like Vienna," *New York Times*, May 23, 2023.

55 Ibid.

56 Kumar Rao, ed., "Building Our Future: Grassroots Reflections on Social Housing," Alliance for Housing Justice, May 2024.

57 Ralph Miliband, *The State in Capitalist Society*, Weidenfeld and Nicolson, 1969, pp. 269–70.

58 Salar Mohandesi, "Faith, or The Stories We Tell," Verso Books (blog) November 8, 2024, versobooks.com.

59 Jalal Movaghary-Pour, "Interview: 'Fight with Hope, Fight without Hope, But Fight Absolutely,'" *London School of Economics' Researching Sociology @LSE Blog*, March 1, 2016, blogs.lsc.ac.uk.

2b. Can We

1 Liza Featherstone, "At a Bleak Political Moment, Zohran Mamdani Offers Hope," *Jacobin*, June 25, 2025.

2 Samuel Stein, *Capital City: Gentrification and the Real Estate State*, Verso, 2019.

3 Jason Epstein, "The Tragical History of New York," *New York Review of Books*, April 9, 1992.

4 Karl Marx, *Capital: Volume III*, Penguin UK, 1992 [1894].

5 Aaron Benanav, *Automation and the Future of Work*, Verso, 2020.

6 Brad Lander, "Comments on New York City's Executive Budget for Fiscal Year 2025 and Financial Plan for Fiscal Years 2024–2028," Office of the New York City Comptroller, comptroller.nyc.gov/reports, May 22, 2024.

7 Francesco Brindisi, Krista Olson, Jonathan Siegel, and Jason Bram, "New York By the Numbers: Monthly Economic and Fiscal Outlook," *Office of the New York City Comptroller*, no. 103 (July 2025).

8 Checkbook NYC, checkbooknyc.com.

9 Lisa Adkins, Melinda Cooper, and Martijn Konings, *The Asset Economy*, John Wiley & Sons, 2020, p. 17.

10 Cooper, *Counterrevolution*.

11 US Department of Labor, Bureau of Labor Statistics, "Union Members – 2024," January 28, 2025.

12 Teresa Ghilarducci, *Labor's Capital: The Economics and Politics of Private Pensions*, MIT Press, 1992.

13 Michael A. McCarthy, *Dismantling Solidarity: Capitalist Politics and American Pensions Since the New Deal*, Cornell University Press, 2017, p. 89.

14 Marnie F. Brady, "Pension Fund Evictions: Lessons for Housing and Labor," PhD diss., Graduate Center of the City University of New York, 2017.

15 Yi-Fu Tuan, *Topophilia: A Study of Environmental Perception, Attitudes, and Values*, Columbia University Press, 1990.

16 David Harvey, "Militant Particularism and Global Ambition: The Conceptual Politics of Place, Space, and Environment in the Work of Raymond Williams," *Social Text* 42, 69–98.

17 Coalition for the Homeless, "Basic Facts About Homelessness in New York City."

18 NYCHA Fact Sheet, 2025.

19 Tatyana Turner, "NYCHA Section 8 Waitlist Applicants Will Soon Learn Their Status," *City Limits,* August 1, 2024.

20 Craig Steven Wilder, *A Covenant with Color: Race and Social Power in Brooklyn 1636–1990*, Columbia University Press, 2000.

21 Joshua Freeman, *Working-Class New York: Life and Labor Since World War II*, The New Press, 2000, p. 114.

22 Roberta Gold, *When Tenants Claimed the City: The Struggle for Citizenship in New York City Housing*, University of Illinois Press, 2014, p. 100.

23 "Title I Protests Mount in Chelsea," *New York Times,* August 24, 1959.

24 Kim Moody, *From Welfare State to Real Estate: Regime Change in New York City, 1974 to the Present*, The New Press, 2007.

25 Samuel Stein and Debipriya Chatterjee, *421-a at 50: Unaffordable New York,* Community Service Society of New York, March 2022.

26 Samuel Stein, "The Art of the Rent Gap," *n+1*, October 25, 2024.

27 James O'Connor, *The Fiscal Crisis of the State*, Routledge, 1973.

28 David Harvey, *A Brief History of Neoliberalism*, Oxford University Press, 2007.

29 Jacob Udell, Celeste Hornbach, Oksana Mironova, and Samuel Stein, "Social Housing and Housing Justice: Pathways to Housing Decommodification," *Law and Political Economy*, May 31, 2022.

30 Samuel Stein, "The Making of Satmar Williamsburg," *Jewish Currents*, November 23, 2021.

31 Kim Stanley Robinson, *New York 2140*, Orbit Books, 2017.

32 M. E. O'Brien and Eman Abdelhadi, *Everything for Everyone: An Oral History of the New York Community, 2052–2072*, Common Notions, 2022.

33 Micah Uetricht, "Amid the Wildfires," *The Nation*, February 9, 2021.

34 Fredric Jameson, "Future City," *New Left Review*, issue 21, May/June 2003.

35 John Maynard Keynes, *A Tract on Monetary Reform*, Cosimo Classics, 1923, p. 80; italics in the original.

36 Naomi Klein, *Doppelganger: A Trip into the Mirror World*, Random House, 2024, p. 321.

37 Stuart Hall, "The Problem of Ideology – Marxism without Guarantees," *Journal of Communication Inquiry* 10, no. 2 (1986): 28–44.

38 Christian M. Anderson, *Urbanism without Guarantees: The Everyday Life of a Gentrifying West Side Neighborhood*, University of Minnesota Press, 2020.

39 Nicos Poulantzas, "Marxist Political Theory in Great Britain," *New Left Review* 43, pp. 73–4.

40 Thomas Angotti and Sylvia Morse, "Preface to the 2023 Edition," in *Zoned Out!: Race, Displacement, and City Planning in New York City (Revised Edition)*, ed. Angotti and Morse, New Village Press, 2023, p. xiii.

41 David Duhalde, "What David Dinkins Taught Us," *Jacobin*, November 25, 2020.

42 Joshua B. Freeman, "How Mayor Fiorello La Guardia Transformed New York City," April 23, 2025.

43 Walter Lippman, "On Municipal Socialism, 1913: An Analysis of Problems and Strategies," in *Socialism and the Cities: Essays by Walter Lippmann and Others,* ed. Bruce M. Stave, Kennikat Press, 1975.

44 Friedrich Engels, *The Housing Question*, Progress Publishers, 1970, p. 69.

45 Sasha Jones, "How New York City Retirees Got Burned by Bets on Rent-Stabilized Apartments," *BisNow,* September 11, 2025.

46 Rosa Luxemburg, *The Mass Strike, the Political Party and the Trade Unions*, Harper and Row, 1971 [1906], p. 17.

47 Rosa Luxemburg, *Reform or Revolution*, Three Arrows Press, 1937 [1908], p. 37.

48 Jane McAlevey, "The Crisis of New Labor and Alinsky's Legacy: Revisiting the Role of the Organic Grassroots Leaders in Building Powerful Organizations and Movements," *Politics & Society* 43, no. 3 (2015): 415–41.

49 Nicole P. Marwell and Paul-Brian McInerney. "The Nonprofit/For-Profit Continuum: Theorizing the Dynamics of Mixed-Form Markets." *Nonprofit and Voluntary Sector Quarterly* 34, no. 1 (2005): 7–28.

50 Ruth Wilson Gilmore, "In the Shadow of the Shadow State," in *The Revolution Will Not Be Funded: Beyond the Non-Profit Industrial Complex*, INCITE! Women of Color Against Violence, Duke University Press, 2007.

51 Alyssa Katz, "The Harm to Affordable Housing," *The American Prospect*, June 28, 2018, pp. 57–9.

52 Cindi Katz, "Partners in Crime? Neoliberalism and the Production of New Political Subjectivities," *Antipode* 37, no. 3 (2005): 623–31.

53 Emily Badger and Quoctrung Bui, "Cities Start to Question an American Ideal: A House with a Yard on Every Lot," *New York Times,* June 18, 2019.
54 J. W. Mason, "What Can Zohran Accomplish?" *Dissent*, July 4, 2025.
55 Patrick M. Condon, *Broken City: Land Speculation, Inequality, and Urban Crisis*, UBC Press, 2024.
56 Ben Morea, *Full Circle: A Life in Rebellion,* Detritus Books, 2025, pp. 160–1.
57 Bruce Robbins, "Optimist Prime," *n+1,* April 29, 2025.
58 New York Senate Bill S6438 and New York Assembly Bill A8281 of the 2019–2020 Legislative Session.
59 Samuel Stein, "Tenants Won This Round," *Jacobin,* June 18, 2019.
60 Celia Weaver, "From Universal Rent Control to Cancel Rent: Tenant Organizing in New York State," *New Labor Forum* 30, no. 1, (2021): pp. 93–8.
61 New York City Department of Housing Preservation & Development, "2021 New York City Housing and Vacancy Survey Selected Initial Findings," May 16, 2022.
62 Francis Fukuyama, "The End of History?," *The National Interest* 16 (1989): 3–18.
63 Mark Fisher, *Capitalist Realism: Is There No Alternative?*, Zer0 Books, 2009.
64 Alexei Yurchak, *Everything Was Forever, Until It Was No More: The Last Soviet Generation,* Princeton University Press, 2013.
65 Antonio Gramsci, as edited and translated by Quintin Hoare and Geoffrey Nowell Smith, *Selections from the Prison Notebooks*, International Publishers, 1992 [1971], p. 276.
66 Ralph Chaplin, "Solidarity Forever," *The International Workers of the World's Little Red Song Book*, 1915.

67 William Callison and Quinn Slobodian, "Coronapolitics from the Reichstag to the Capital," *Boston Review*, January 12, 2021.

68 William F. Buckley, "Our Mission Statement," *The National Review,* November 19, 1955.

69 Walter Benjamin, "Paralipomena to 'On the Concept of History,'" *Walter Benjamin Selected Writings* vol. 4, ed. Michael W. Jennings et al., Harvard University Press, 2006, p. 402. As quoted in Salar Mohandesi, "Faith, or The Stories We Tell,'" Verso Books (blog), November 8, 2024, versobooks.com.

70 Colin Gorenstein, "Ta-Nehisi Coates Tells Jon Stewart That America's Optimism Is Misplaced: The Arc of History 'Bends Toward Chaos,'" *Salon*, July 24, 2015.

71 Samuel Hunter, *A Bright New Boise*, Samuel French, 2012.

72 Ujju Aggarwal, *Unsettling Choice: Race, Rights, and the Partitioning of Public Education*, University of Minnesota Press, 2024.

73 *The Guardian,* "Margaret Thatcher: A Life in Quotes," April 8, 2013.

74 David Graeber, "Of Flying Cars and the Declining Rate of Profit," *The Baffler,* no. 19 (March 2012); Pascal-Emanuel Gobry, "Facebook Investor Wants Flying Cars, Not 140 Characters," *Business Insider,* July 30, 2011.

75 Vivian Gornick, *The Romance of American Communism*, Tantor and Blackstone, 1977.

76 Max Elbaum, *Revolution in the Air: Sixties Radicals Turn to Lenin, Mao and Che*, Verso, 2018.

77 M. Gessen, *Where the Jews Aren't: The Sad and Absurd Story of Birobidzhan, Russia's Jewish Autonomous Region*, Schocken, 2016.

78 Bini Adamczak, *Yesterday's Tomorrow: On the Loneliness of Communist Specters and the Reconstruction of the Future*, MIT Press, 2021, pp. 78–9.

79 Raphael Magarik, “Parshat Naso,” *Jewish Currents,* June 6, 2025.

80 Andy Battle, “Runaway: A History of Postwar New York in Four Factories,” PhD diss., City University of New York, 2019.

81 Walter Benjamin, “Left-Wing Melancholy,” in *The Weimar Republic Sourcebook*, ed. Anton Kaes, Martin Jay, and Edward Dimendberg, University of California Press, 1994, p. 305.

82 Enzo Traverso, *Left-Wing Melancholia: Marxism, History, and Memory*, Columbia University Press, 2016.

83 Mariame Kaba, *We Do This ‘Til We Free Us: Abolitionist Organizing and Transforming Justice*, Haymarket Books, 2021, p. 26.

3. Doubt and Faith

1 An abridged version of the sermon was published as: Rabbi Miriam Grossman, “Let’s Build a Room for Hope,” *Lilith,* October 19, 2023.